JONI SEAGER is a Canadian feminist geographer and a university lecturer in Geography, Women's Studies and International Development. She is co-director of the Association of American Geographers' Specialist Group on Women and is Coordinator of Women's Studies at MIT.

ANN OLSON is an American geographer and cartographer and a feminist. She has worked for the United States Geological Survey on the US National Atlas and for the United Nations University on the Mountain Hazards Mapping Project.

WOMEN
IN THE
WORLD
AN INTERNATIONAL ATLAS

JONI SEAGER & ANN OLSON

A PLUTO PRESS PROJECT

Edited by Michael Kidron

A TOUCHSTONE BOOK
PUBLISHED BY SIMON & SCHUSTER, INC. NEW YORK

Simon and Schuster/Touchstone Books,
Published by Simon & Schuster, Inc.
Simon & Schuster Building,
Rockefeller Center,
1230 Avenue of the Americas
New York, New York 10020

SIMON AND SCHUSTER, TOUCHSTONE and colophons are registered trademarks of Simon & Schuster, Inc.

Designed by Tilly Northedge of Grundy & Northedge, London
Artwork by Swanston Graphics, Derby
Cover illustration by Stuart Bodek
Coordinated by Anne Benewick

Color origination by Imago Publishing Ltd
Printed and bound in Hong Kong by Mandarin Offset International (HK) Ltd

1 2 3 4 5 6 7 8 9 10 (hardback)
1 2 3 4 5 6 7 8 9 10 (paperback)

Library of Congress Cataloging in Publication Data

Seager, Joni

Women in the world.

1. Women – Social conditions. 2. Women – Economic conditions. 3. Women.
I. Olson, Ann. II. Title. HQ1154.03965 1986 305.4'2 86-6739

ISBN 0-671-60297-7 (hardback)
    0-671-63070-9 (paperback)

CONTENTS

CONTENTS

Most women in the world, like most men, lead humble lives. Their daily preoccupations are with economic survival and success, raising healthy and happy children, making sure that personal and family needs are met, and garnering some measure of emotional satisfaction from life. What is striking, though, is how different women's ordinary lives are from men's ordinary lives. And to see women's lives we cannot simply look at the world of men and proceed to women as an afterthought.

This atlas rests on the assumption that we cannot understand our world without understanding the everyday experience of women. Women's contributions are at least as important as those of men: 'They are the providers of food, fuel, water, and often the whole family income – the sustainers and developers of their families, communities, and countries . . . the fate of women is a critical determinant of the fate of whole societies.' (Margaret Snyder, UN Voluntary Fund for Women)

In this atlas, we ask not only *what* is happening between women and men (and between women themselves), but *where* it is happening. Geography matters, we believe. By mapping the world of women, patterns are revealed that are usually obscured in statistical tables or in narratives. The similarities and differences, the continuities and contrasts among women around the world are best shown by – literally – mapping out their lives. Although maps suggest objectivity, no atlas is free from a point of view; our feminism legitimately informs our work. We do not presume a global community of women. What we do see, however, is that everywhere women are worse off than men: women have less power, less autonomy, more work, less money, and more responsibility. Women everywhere have a smaller share of the pie; if the pie is very small (as in poor countries), women's share is smaller still. Women in rich countries have a higher standard of living than do women in poor countries, but nowhere are women equal to men.

There are other commonalities, formed from common experiences. Women everywhere share primary responsibility for having and rearing children, for forming and maintaining families, for contraception. They share, too, the lead in fighting for women's rights, for other civil rights, and for peace. Rich and poor, they also suffer rape, health traumas from illegal abortions, the degradation of pornography.

Nevertheless, global generalizations are not meant to obscure the very real differences that exist between women, country by country, region by region. For example:

- In Afghanistan four per cent of eligible girls are enrolled in secondary school; in Australia 88 per cent are;

- In Angola fewer than one per cent of adult women have access to contraceptives; in Belgium 76 per cent do;

7

- Women in Ghana bear an average of over six children; women in West Germany, fewer than two;
- In Jamaica the maternal mortality rate stands at 106 mothers' deaths for every 100,000 births; in Norway there are fewer than 8 deaths per 100,000 births.

Inequalities in wealth and access to opportunities should not be minimized. In poor countries (usually described as the 'Third World' or the 'developing' world – labels we have tried to avoid), most people are in a situation of dependency, powerlessness, vulnerability and inequality of income. All of these conditions of 'under-development' are experienced by women to a greater extent. Yet the distinction between the 'First' and 'Third' worlds is usually made on the basis of economic indicators which often have little to do with women's lives, and that do not necessarily help to assess their situation and status. In fact, looking at the world through women's eyes raises questions about the validity of conventional distinctions between 'developed' and 'underdeveloped' countries:

- In both Saudi Arabia and Austria women make up less than 20 per cent of university teachers, but almost 100 per cent of pre-primary school teachers;
- In Haiti women constitute five per cent of all employees in the media; in Japan two per cent;
- In Peru and Canada, in the UK and Uruguay, women have the same proportion of representation in government;
- The governments in Romania and Chad have similarly repressive population policies, restricting women's access to contraceptives and family planning.

In the world of women there are few 'developed' nations.

But women's lives are not fully captured by bleak statistics. Over the past two decades there have been tremendous advances in education for women. More and more women are being paid to work. Governments are being pressured to recognize and protect women's rights. But most importantly and positively, women are coming out of the shadows and fighting for what is rightfully theirs. It is independent organizing on the part of women that has given us equal opportunity laws, the right to abortion, and battered-women's shelters.

There are few instances where men in authority have shared power with women voluntarily. Women have not automatically gained through national struggles or under 'revolutionary' governments: a rising tide does not necessarily raise all boats, and women have frequently been left behind even when broad social advances have been made. The attitudes of men in power to women seem to be remarkably similar across a wide geographic and political spectrum. Within one month in the autumn of 1985 the newspapers reported the words of a high ranking American official: 'women don't understand the issues at the peace summit ... or what is happening in human rights'; the Greek president exhorting women to have more babies to help bolster military manpower to face a future threat from Turkey; and President Marcos of the Philippines saying that he was 'embarrassed' to be running in a political campaign against a woman.

This world atlas of women not only explores the similarities and differences between and among women – it also raises fundamental questions about who has authority, who has power and who does not, who is on top and who is at the bottom. We have tried to capture the world of women within as broad a reach as possible. Maps in the chapters on *Marriage* and *Motherhood* consider not only the act of marriage, but also some of its consequences – which include domestic violence and early death in childbirth. In *Work*, unpaid work in the household, universally considered to be women's work, is contrasted with the share of paid work done by women. Under *Resources* and *Welfare*, we map health and education, women refugees, and global trends toward the feminization of poverty. We look at *Authority* in the World: in governments, in the militaries, and in the media. Prostitution, rape, and beauty contests are dealt with in *Body Politics*. In the section on *Change*, we have tried to capture the various ways in which women forge social change – on their own behalf and for others.

Each map-spread focuses on a central topic, and usually includes two or three sub-topics supporting the main one. A short text provides a brief introduction and draws attention to the inter-relationships between the graphics. Comments and background information are provided in the notes. We have also tried to include here information that we could not find space for on the maps – so the notes also form a separate resource section.

Throughout the research for this atlas we have been hampered by the inadequacy and inaccessibility of international data on women. *Some* information exists on almost all topics but, with the exception of a few standard indicators, information on women is conspicuously absent from conventional sources. A large share of the data in this book was gleaned from feminist writing in small presses, newsletters from women's organizations the world over, and 'alternative' journals of various descriptions: this makes for interesting reading, but laborious research. For all maps, multiple sources (an average of more than ten per map) were used to cross-check reliability and to fill in uneven information patterns.

The official invisibility of women perpetuates the myth that what women do is less important, less noteworthy, less significant. Women are *made* invisible by policies and priorities that discount the importance of collecting information about them. Although the United Nations Decade for Women (1975–85) resulted in a considerable increase in international information on women, women are still not generally included in the information mainstream. Largely as a result of these data constraints, there are a number of topics that we consider important but could not include. Readers will notice that large areas of interest, such as women and religion, and women and shelter, are missing. We do not offer information about women in sports, or women in the arts. We have nothing to map on lesbians or disabled women. We can do little about these omissions except to note them, and to assure readers that they are not an indication of disregard on our part.

The planning for this atlas took two years, the research another year and a half. Over this time our understanding of the issues that affect women, and of the importance of making international comparisons, has deepened. We have often been struck by the realization that women's lives are complex, and it is never simple to draw comparisons across cultures. As Western, white women, we have struggled with our own limitations in understanding the experiences of women in a very wide and diverse world. Primarily, though, we have been heartened by the examples of women coping, women changing, and women solving their own problems. In the world of women, things are both better and worse than one might think.

There are many people without whom this atlas would not have appeared:

Mike Kidron, our editor, put in long hours and hard work editing the sometimes incomprehensible manuscripts we sent – and he did so with much creativity and in good humour; to him also goes full credit for initiating and overseeing the entire atlas series. Anne Benewick coordinated all of the production – a monumental task on a project such as this – and added a voice of reason when the rest of us were becoming unreasonable. Tilly Northedge designed all of the wonderful graphics and displays that make this atlas so exceptional. Nina Kidron provided support, substantial insight, and kept us on the books. Cynthia Enloe and Dan Smith provided the initial introduction to Pluto Press. Angela Quinn provided editorial assistance during the early stages.

Ed Deagle and Alberta Arthurs at the Rockefeller Foundation deserve a lot of credit, and our sincere thanks, for going out of their way to support a somewhat unorthodox proposal; Alison Bernstein shepherded our funding requests through the Ford Foundation. It was the financial support from these two foundations that allowed us to undertake the full-time research for this book.

The Institute for Policy Studies (Washington DC) and the Wellesley College Center for Research on Women (Wellesley, Massachusetts) provided institutional support. Our special thanks to Bob Borosage, Nancy Lewis and Doris Porter at IPS, and to Laura Lein and Jan Putnam at Wellesley.

Our advisory board lent their good names and support to this unlikely venture. Much appreciation to: Elise Boulding; Barbara Ehrenreich; Cynthia Enloe; Rayna Green; Perdita Huston; Mildred Marcy; Joann Vanek.

Christopher Laxton supported the project with his love and assistance, editorial and computing insight, and skilful baby care – and helped in the creation of another wonderful project, Sarah Lindsay. Cynthia Enloe offered constant encouragement, unqualified support . . . and considerable data.

Our most substantial debt is to countless unnamed feminists who, for years, have been the only ones insisting that it is important to ask questions about where the women are. Without the collective support of the women's movement, and the pathbreaking efforts of a persistent few, we would have neither the knowledge nor the confidence to undertake this atlas.

And lastly, but certainly not least, our thanks to each other. It is our friendship and our faith in each other that kept us going through the three years of this project.

Joni Seager
Ann Olson

London, January 1986

ACKNOWLEDGEMENTS

Many people and organizations in addition to those already acknowledged contributed data, encouragement and advice. Without their help this atlas would be substantially shorter. Our thanks to:

Anne Marie Amantia, Population Crisis Committee, Washington DC; American College of Nurse Midwives, Washington DC; American Home Economics Association, Washington DC; Alice Andrews, George Mason University; Rita Arditti, FINNRAGE (Feminist International Network of Resistance to Reproductive and Genetic Engineering); Arlington County Public Library, Central Library, Reference Staff; Kathleen Barry, International Feminist Network Against Female Sexual Slavery; Jade Blaney, Stratford, Ontario; Philippa Brewster, London; Judith Bruce, Population Council, New York City; Gilda Bruckman, Boston; Ximena Bunster, Santiago; Canadian-American Center, University of Maine; Carol Carp, American Public Health Association, Washington DC; Miriam Chamberlain, National Council for Research on Women, New York City; Antoinette Clancy, Women's Political Party, Ireland; Paul Clarke, Reston, Virginia; Dean Cooke, Toronto; Mona Domosh, Worcester, Massachusetts; Renate Duelli Klein, FINNRAGE; Tracy Enright, Pan American Health Organization, Washington DC; Equity Policy Center, Washington DC; Maria Estroza, Pan American Health Organization, Washington DC; Feminist International Network of Resistance to Reproductive and Genetic Engineering (FINNRAGE); Elena Fletcher, National Cancer Institute, Bethesda, Maryland.

Jill Gay, Institute for Policy Studies, Washington DC; Elizabeth Grant, Delegation of the Commission of the European Communities, New York; Barbara Haber, Schlesinger Library, Radcliffe College; Susan Hanson, Clark University; Sandra Harding, University of Delaware; Jane Hawksley, London; Fran Hosken, Women's International Network, Lexington, Massachusetts; Jaimie Hubbard, Toronto; International Labor Organization, Geneva and Washington DC; International Planned Parenthood Federation, New York City and London; Constant Jacquet, National Council of Churches; Evelina Kane, Women Against Pornography, New York City; Jeanne Kasperson, CENTED, Clark University; Doris Krebs, International Council of Nurses; David Lee, National Clearinghouse on Marital Rape; London Rape Crisis Centre; Helen MacSherry, United Nations Information Center, Washington DC; Mike McDermott, Reston, Virginia; Peggy McIntosh, Wellesley College Center for Research on Women; Minority Rights Group, London; Janice Monk, Southwest Institute for Research on Women, Tucson, Arizona; Moynihan's Bar, Worcester, Massachusetts; Aimee Nestingen, Pan American Health Organization, Washington DC.

Office of Women in Development, Agency for International Development, Washington DC; Jon Olson, Pasadena, California; Mary M. Olson, Washington DC; Peter Olson, Arlington, Virginia; William C. Olson, American University; Phyllis Palmer, Women's Studies Program, George Washington University; Deborah Pearlman, Brandeis University; Population Reference Bureau, Library staff; April Powers, Institute for Policy Studies, Washington DC; Betty Reardon, Teacher's College, Columbia University; Caryn Riley, International Labor Organization, Washington DC; Keven Roth, Herndor, Virginia; Lois Roth, Washington DC; E. Royston, Division of Family Health, World Health Organization; Bob Schaaf, Library of Congress, Washington DC; Joan Seager, Toronto; Julie Seager, Nassau; Ruth Sivard, World Priorities, Washington DC; Barbara Sloan, Delegation of the Commission of the European Communities; Sian Steward, Boston; Wendy Stickel, Agency for International Development; Norma Swenson, Boston Women's Healthbook Collective; United States Geological Survey; Judith Wachs, Boston; Anne Walker, International Women's Tribune Center, New York City; Betsy Warrior, Boston; Lois Wasserspring, Wellesley College; Barbara Wein, World Policy Institute, New York City; Wellesley College, Reference Library staff; Karen White, International Center for Research on Women; Women's Institute for Freedom of the Press, Washington DC; World Health Organization; Laura X, National Clearinghouse on Marital Rape.

SECOND IN RIGHTS

Constitutional provisions for women's rights and equality, 1985

Legend: date of latest provision in any area | **=** in general sexual equality | **O** in marriage and the family | **↘** in employment

AFRICA

Country	Date	=	O	↘
Algeria	1976	=		
Benin	1979		O	
Botswana	1971	=		
Burkina Faso	1970	=		
Burundi	1981	=		
Cameroon	1975	=		
Cape Verde	1980	=		
CAR	1981	=		↘
Comoros	1978	=		
Congo	1979	=		↘
Djibouti	1977	=		
Egypt	1980			
Equatorial Guinea	1982	=	O	
Gabon	1982	=		↘
Gambia	1970	=		
Guinea	1982			
Ivory Coast	1975	=		
Kenya	1979	=		
Liberia	1983	=		↘
Madagascar	1975	=		
Mauritania	1978			
Mauritius	1977	=		
Morocco	1972			
Mozambique	1975	=		
Rwanda	1978	=		
Sao Tome and Principe	1975	=		
Senegal	1981	=		
Seychelles	1979			
Sierra Leone	1978	=		
Somalia	1979	=		↘
Sudan	1973	=		↘
Tanzania	1977	=		
Togo	1979	=		
Tunisia	1976			
Uganda	1967			
Zaire	1978	=		↘
Zambia	1979	=		
Zimbabwe	1979	=		

AMERICAS

Country	Date	=	O	↘
Antigua and Barbuda	1981	=		
Argentina	1968			
Bahamas	1973	=		
Barbados	1966	=		
Belize	1981	=		
Bolivia	1967	=	O	
Brazil	1982	=		↘
Canada	1985	=		
Chile	1980			
Costa Rica	1977		O	↘
Cuba	1976	=	O	↘
Dominica	1978	=		
Dominican Republic	1966			
Ecuador	1978	=	O	
El Salvador	1962			↘
Guatemala	1982	=		↘
Guyana	1980	=		↘
Haiti	1964		O	
Honduras	1982	=	O	↘
Jamaica	1962			
Mexico	1981	=		↘
Nicaragua	1979	=	O	↘
Panama	1979	=	O	↘
Paraguay	1977			
Peru	1979	=		↘
St Kitts-Nevis	1983	=		
St Lucia	1978	=		
St Vincent	1979	=		
Surinam	1982	=	O	↘
USA	1967			
Uruguay	1966			
Venezuela	1961	=		↘

ASIA AND OCEANIA

Country	Date	=	O	↘
Afghanistan	1978	=		
Bahrain	1973			
Burma	1981	=	O	
China	1982	=	O	↘
Fiji	1970	=		
India	1979	=		
Indonesia	1945			
Iraq	1970	=		
Israel	1951		O	
Japan	1947	=	O	
Jordan	1952			
Kiribati	1979	=		
Korea, North	1972	=		
Korea, South	1980	=	O	
Lebanon	1947			
Malaysia	1981			
Maldives	1975			
Mongolia	1980	=		↘
Nauru	1968	=		
Nepal	1978	=		
New Zealand	1977			↘
Pakistan	1981	=		
Papua New Guinea	1978	=		
Qatar	1972	=		
Singapore	1980			
Solomon Islands	1978	=		
Sri Lanka	1978	=		
Syria	1973			↘
Taiwan	1947	=		
Thailand	1978			
Tonga	1981			
Tuvalu	1978	=		
United Arab Emirates	1971			
USSR	1977	=	O	↘
Vanuatu	1979	=		
Vietnam	1980	=	O	↘
Western Samoa	1981	=		
Yemen, North	1970	=		
Yemen, South	1970			

EUROPE

Country	Date	=	O	↘
Albania	1976	=	O	↘
Austria	1974	=		
Belgium	1971			
Bulgaria	1971	=	O	
Cyprus	1960	=		
Czechoslovakia	1960	=	O	↘
Finland	1981			
France	1963			
Germany, East	1974	=	O	↘
Germany, West	1973	=		
Greece	1975	=		↘
Hungary	1972	=		↘
Ireland	1979			
Italy	1947	=	O	↘
Lichtenstein	1965			
Luxembourg	1956			
Malta	1974	=		↘
Monaco	1962			
Netherlands	1983	=		
Poland	1976	=		↘
Portugal	1982	=	O	↘
Romania	1975	=		↘
Spain	1978	=	O	↘
Sweden	1975	=		
Switzerland	1981			↘
Turkey	1982	=		
Yugoslavia	1974	=		
United Kingdom	1975	=	O	↘

For women, there are no developed countries. Although some places are clearly better for them to live in than others, it is not always true that the relatively rich countries of the world provide better circumstances for them as women than do poorer countries.

While many countries provide formally for sexual equality in law, very few governments have legislated to protect specific job and marriage rights; and such law as exists is nullified or blunted in its effect by social and administrative practice. Nowhere do women have full equal rights with men.

Yet women are biologically stronger, live longer than men, and naturally outnumber them. Where they do not, it is only because of the effects of war, or because they have been forced to migrate in search of work, or because they have suffered severe and systematic discrimination.

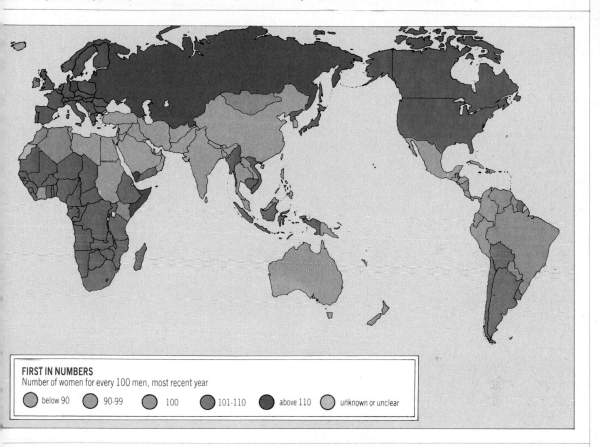

FIRST IN NUMBERS
Number of women for every 100 men, most recent year

○ below 90   ○ 90-99   ○ 100   ○ 101-110   ○ above 110   ○ unknown or unclear

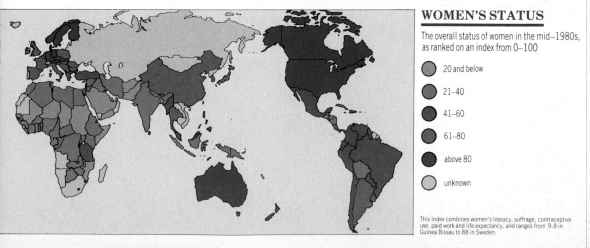

WOMEN'S STATUS

The overall status of women in the mid–1980s, as ranked on an index from 0–100

○ 20 and below

○ 21–40

○ 41–60

○ 61–80

○ above 80

○ unknown

This index combines women's literacy, suffrage, contraceptive use, paid work and life expectancy, and ranges from 9.8 in Guinea Bissau to 88 in Sweden.

Sources in Notes

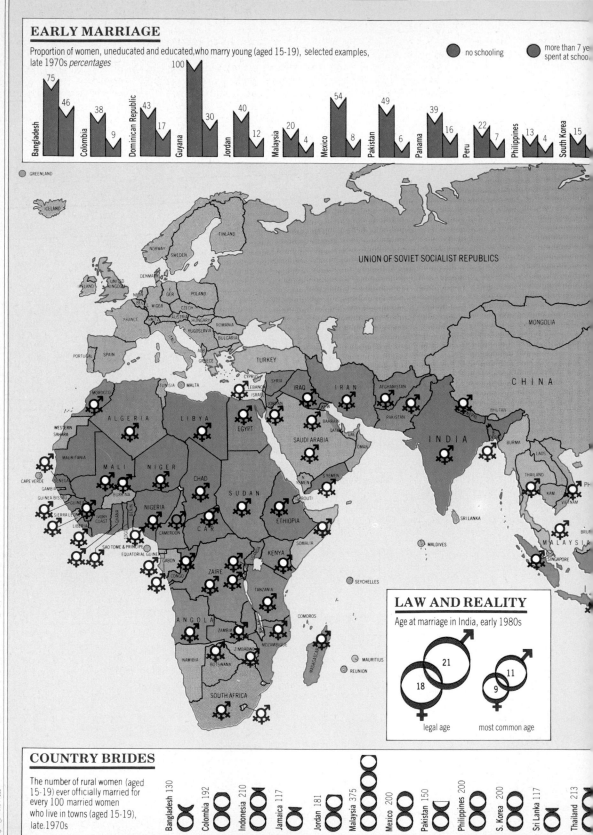

EARLY MARRIAGE

Proportion of women, uneducated and educated, who marry young (aged 15-19), selected examples, late 1970s *percentages*

● no schooling ● more than 7 ye
spent at schoo

Bangladesh 75 46
Colombia 38 9
Dominican Republic 43 17
Guyana 100 30
Jordan 40 12
Malaysia 20 4
Mexico 54 8
Pakistan 49 6
Panama 39 16
Peru 22 7
Philippines 13 4
South Korea 15

UNION OF SOVIET SOCIALIST REPUBLICS

CHINA

MONGOLIA

INDIA

LAW AND REALITY

Age at marriage in India, early 1980s

21 18 11 9

legal age most common age

COUNTRY BRIDES

The number of rural women (aged 15-19) ever officially married for every 100 married women who live in towns (aged 15-19), late 1970s

Bangladesh 130
Colombia 192
Indonesia 210
Jamaica 117
Jordan 181
Malaysia 375
Mexico 200
Pakistan 150
Philippines 200
S. Korea 200
Sri Lanka 117
Thailand 213

Most women and men in the world spend most of their lives as married people, but for women this is a way of life.

Marriage grants women adult status. But many women marry while themselves still children. Early marriages bring many hardships, resulting in many more births, less autonomy, and a greater likelihood of being widowed in mid-life.

Even though legal age minimums for marriage are rising everywhere, youthful weddings still take place, because marrying-off adolescent daughters rids older parents of useless cargo; because in many places there is no role for a single woman in society; and because other older men value young wives – for their virginity and social status.

Women marry youngest in the country, where there are fewer opportunities for independence and change than in the city.

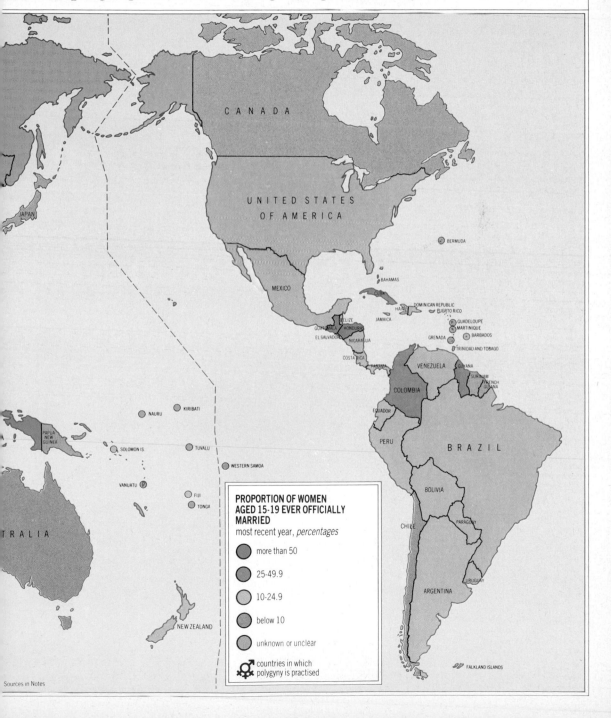

PROPORTION OF WOMEN AGED 15-19 EVER OFFICIALLY MARRIED
most recent year, *percentages*

- more than 50
- 25-49.9
- 10-24.9
- below 10
- unknown or unclear

⚥ countries in which polygyny is practised

SHELTERS: THE FIRST TEN YEARS

Year in which first women's shelter was opened

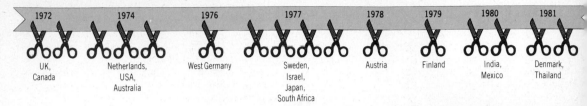

1972	1974	1976	1977	1978	1979	1980	1981
UK, Canada	Netherlands, USA, Australia	West Germany	Sweden, Israel, Japan, South Africa	Austria	Finland	India, Mexico	Denmark, Thailand

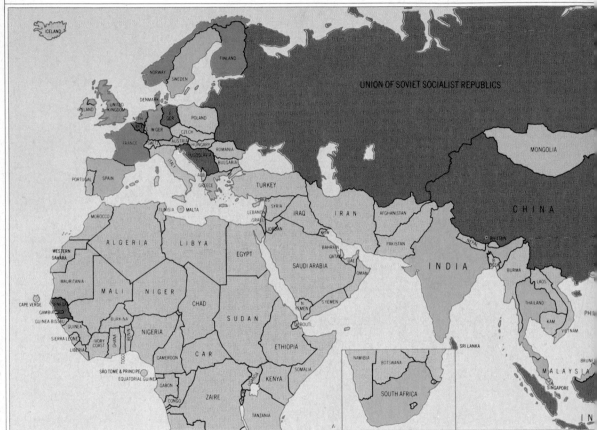

SECOND BEST

The preference for sons or daughters, in 27 countries, 1980s

♂ son   ♀ daughter

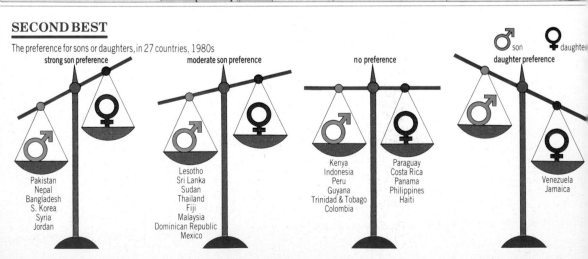

strong son preference

Pakistan
Nepal
Bangladesh
S. Korea
Syria
Jordan

moderate son preference

Lesotho
Sri Lanka
Sudan
Thailand
Fiji
Malaysia
Dominican Republic
Mexico

no preference

Kenya
Indonesia
Peru
Guyana
Trinidad & Tobago
Colombia

Paraguay
Costa Rica
Panama
Philippines
Haiti

daughter preference

Venezuela
Jamaica

DOMESTIC DISORDERS 3

Men of all classes and countries use violence and coercion to 'keep women in their place'. Millions of women are beaten each year in their homes; many are killed. Some cultures encourage wife-beating as a man's right; in others, the problem is hidden away as a 'private' matter. There is little official recognition of this violence; but women throughout the world are organizing against it, and battered women's shelters now exist in many countries.

In Islamic states, the veiling and seclusion of women serve to keep them dependent on their husbands and exclusive to them. There is a current resurgence in the observance and enforcement of veiling practices; in two countries, the veil is compulsory for women in public.

Domestic coercion stems from the fact that in most countries women are considered to be men's property, and girls are less valued than boys.

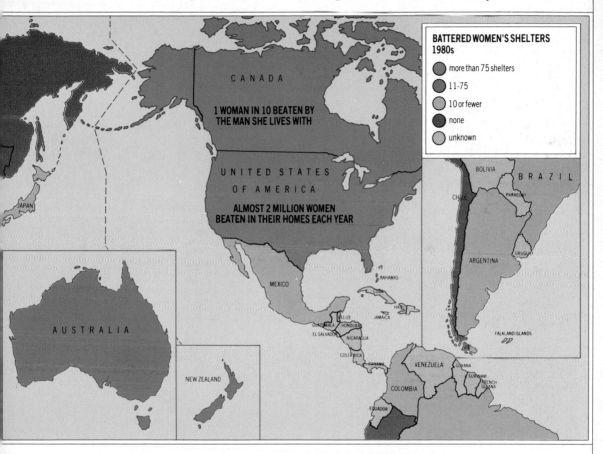

BATTERED WOMEN'S SHELTERS 1980s
- more than 75 shelters
- 11–75
- 10 or fewer
- none
- unknown

CANADA
1 WOMAN IN 10 BEATEN BY THE MAN SHE LIVES WITH

UNITED STATES OF AMERICA
ALMOST 2 MILLION WOMEN BEATEN IN THEIR HOMES EACH YEAR

KEEPING WOMEN IN THEIR PLACE

Veiling of women in countries where over 50 per cent of the population is Muslim

- compulsory
- most women veiled
- some women veiled
- few women veiled
- other Islamic countries
- other countries
- seclusion is accepted practice

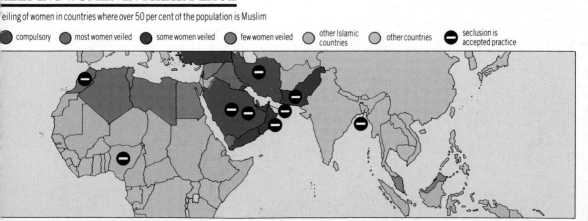

84 MILLION MUTILATED WOMEN

Proportion of women and girls excised and infibulated, where known, Africa 1982, *percentages*

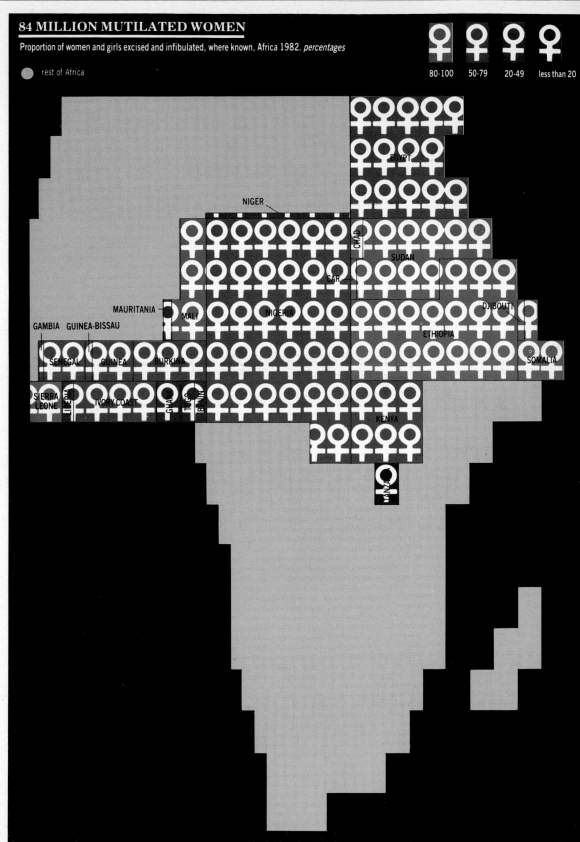

rest of Africa

80-100   50-79   20-49   less than 20

Sources in Notes

Female genital mutilation – female circumcision as it is sometimes called – is extensively practised in Africa and the Middle East. It may be performed by older village women on babies as young as a few days old or on girls in their late adolescence. The 'operation' is rarely performed with surgical tools or skill any knowledge of anatomy or the use of anaesthesia.

Reasons given for the operation are varied, but wherever it is practised, it prepares girls for marriage by helping to ensure their premarital purity. It lessens sexual desire, and so reduces the temptation for girls and women to have intercourse before marriage – very important where virginity is an absolute prerequisite for a bride-to-be.

Genital mutilation is justified in other ways too. Some Moslem groups believe it is demanded by the Islamic faith (and only Moslems practise infibulation). Other groups hold erroneous beliefs about human biology and use circumcision as contraception. In some cultures, female genitals are considered unclean, and circumcision serves literally to smooth and ritually purify them.

Genital mutilation has staggering physical and mental health consequences for women. Infections (frequently fatal), haemorrhage, and other extreme long-term physical complications, are common. The extent and degree of sexual and mental health problems can only be guessed at, though, because circumcised women are often hesitant to discuss a subject that means little to them or is embarrassing: their sexuality. In spite of growing worldwide concern about genital mutilation, the practice is not yet declining.

Female circumcision is practised in the West, sometimes surreptitiously, but occurrences are sporadic and undocumented.

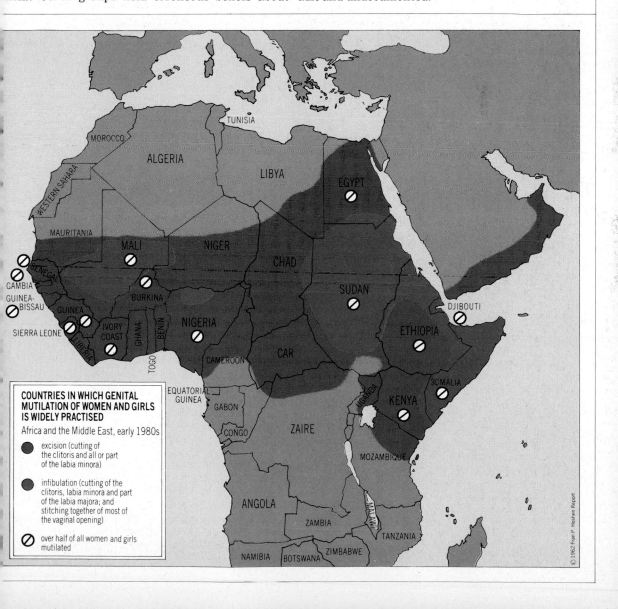

COUNTRIES IN WHICH GENITAL MUTILATION OF WOMEN AND GIRLS IS WIDELY PRACTISED

Africa and the Middle East, early 1980s

- excision (cutting of the clitoris and all or part of the labia minora)

- infibulation (cutting of the clitoris, labia minora and part of the labia majora; and stitching together of most of the vaginal opening)

- Ø over half of all women and girls mutilated

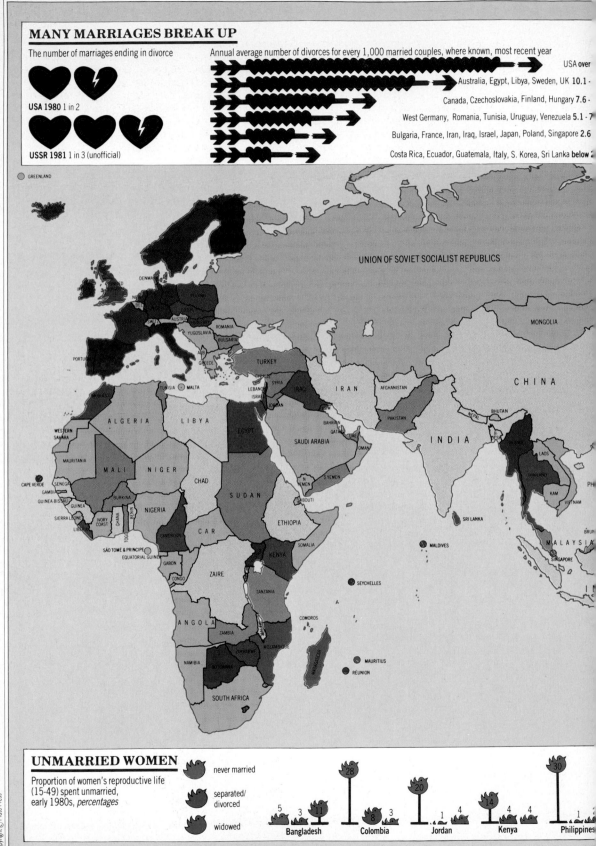

MANY MARRIAGES BREAK UP

The number of marriages ending in divorce

Annual average number of divorces for every 1,000 married couples, where known, most recent year

USA over

Australia, Egypt, Libya, Sweden, UK **10.1 -**

Canada, Czechoslovakia, Finland, Hungary **7.6 -**

West Germany, Romania, Tunisia, Uruguay, Venezuela **5.1 - 7**

Bulgaria, France, Iran, Iraq, Israel, Japan, Poland, Singapore **2.6**

Costa Rica, Ecuador, Guatemala, Italy, S. Korea, Sri Lanka **below 2**

USA 1980 1 in 2

USSR 1981 1 in 3 (unofficial)

UNION OF SOVIET SOCIALIST REPUBLICS

GREENLAND

DENMARK

POLAND

AUSTRIA

ROMANIA

YUGOSLAVIA

BULGARIA

ALB

GREECE

PORTU

TUNISIA • MALTA

CYPRUS

SYRIA

LEBANON

ISRAEL

JORDAN

TURKEY

IRAQ

IRAN

AFGHANISTAN

MONGOLIA

CHINA

WESTERN SAHARA

ALGERIA

LIBYA

EGYPT

MAURITANIA

MALI

NIGER

CHAD

SUDAN

SAUDI ARABIA

BAHRAIN

QATAR UAE

OMAN

PAKISTAN

NEPAL

BHUTAN

B. DESH

INDIA

LAOS

CAPE VERDE

SENEGAL

GAMBIA

GUINEA-BISSAU

GUINEA

SIERRA LEONE

LIBERIA

IVORY COAST

GHANA

BURKINA

TOGO

BENIN

NIGERIA

CAMEROON

CAR

ETHIOPIA

N. YEMEN

YEMEN

DJIBOUTI

SOMALIA

KAM

VIETNAM

THAILAND

PH

SÃO TOMÉ & PRINCIPE

EQUATORIAL GUINEA

GABON

CONGO

ZAIRE

KENYA

TANZANIA

SEYCHELLES

MALDIVES

SRI LANKA

MALAYSIA

SINGAPORE

BRUN

ANGOLA

ZAMBIA

ZIMBABWE

MOZAMBIQUE

COMOROS

MADAGASCAR

MAURITIUS

RÉUNION

NAMIBIA

BOTSWANA

SOUTH AFRICA

UNMARRIED WOMEN

Proportion of women's reproductive life
(15-49) spent unmarried,
early 1980s, *percentages*

never married

separated/divorced

widowed

	Bangladesh	Colombia	Jordan	Kenya	Philippines
never married	5	28	20	30	
separated/divorced	3	8 3	1 4	14 4 4	1
widowed	11				

Women marry for a variety of reasons: economic security, social status, and emotional wellbeing. But women who don't marry are often viewed as failures, even pariahs, and frequently see themselves that way.

Worst off by far are women once married, now single. The social status of widows and divorcees can be very low. In some cultures, widows are not even allowed to remarry; thus losing their one possible route back to security.

Divorce is not a universal right for men, much less for women. In most Muslim countries, a man can divorce simply by declaring his intentions, while his wife has no right to divorce at all.

Divorce is a mixed blessing for women: this important right can leave women and children worse off financially, while their ex-husbands gain. Divorce is increasing worldwide – for better or for worse.

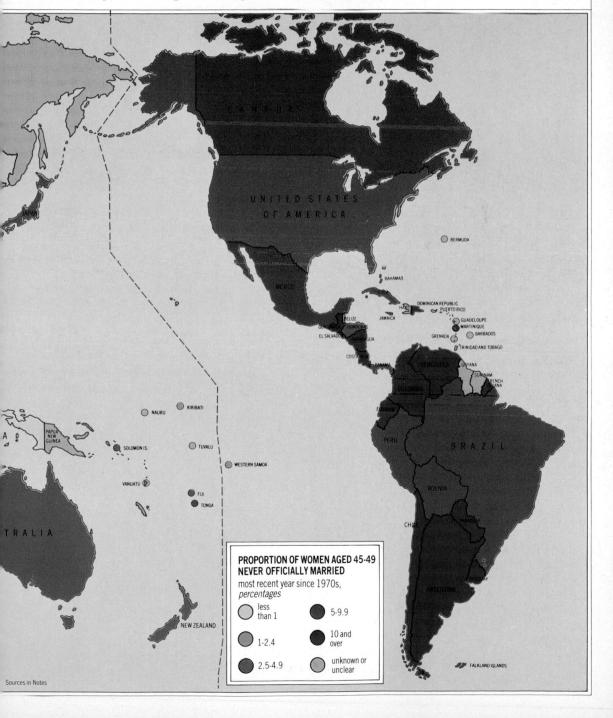

PROPORTION OF WOMEN AGED 45-49 NEVER OFFICIALLY MARRIED

most recent year since 1970s, *percentages*

- less than 1
- 1-2.4
- 2.5-4.9
- 5-9.9
- 10 and over
- unknown or unclear

MANY WAYS TO BE MOTHERS

Births to mothers who are single or in a union other than 'official marriage' as a proportion of all births, Caribbean, where known, early 1980s, *percentages*

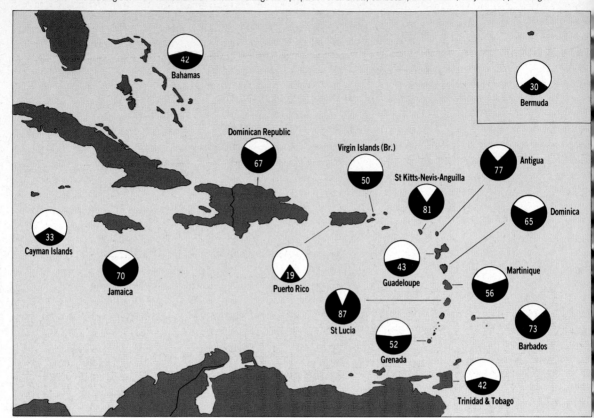

TEENAGE MOTHERS

Births to women under 20 years old as a proportion of all births, latest available year since 1970s, *percentages*

over 20   11-20   5-10   below 5   unknown or unclear

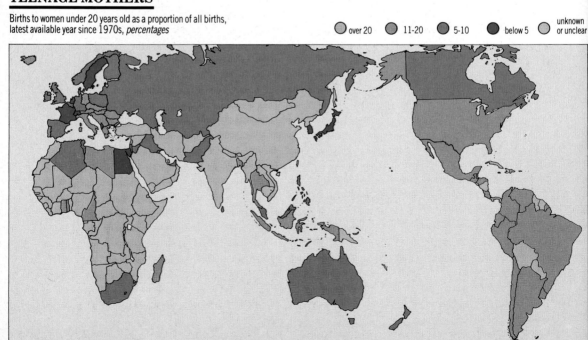

Childbirth is one of the few true universals in women's lives. Women are the ones who bear children, a fact that is used everywhere to construct theories and institutions which define, limit, and dictate their roles in society.

But the conditions of pregnancy and motherhood vary widely. In some countries, women have an average of seven children; in others, fewer than two. This is the result of different population policies,

varying standards of health and wealth, differing pressures from men who often see their manhood affirmed by the number of children they father, and the degree of autonomy accorded to women.

Many teenage women have children – as young brides, or as single mothers. Many women, in some places the majority, have children when single or in consensual unions. Official marital status has little influence on women's childbearing experiences.

TOTAL FERTILITY RATE

Average number of children women bear, early 1980s
extremes: West Germany 1.4 - Kenya, Zimbabwe above 8.0

⬤ below 2   ⬤ 2.0-4.0   ⬤ 4.1-6.0   ⬤ above 6   ⬤ unknown or unclear

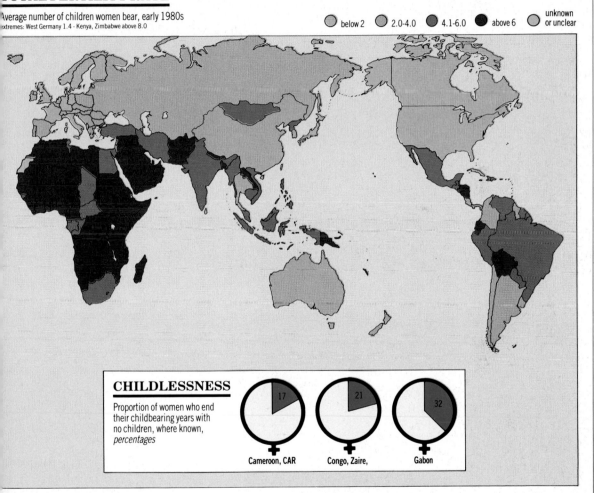

CHILDLESSNESS

Proportion of women who end their childbearing years with no children, where known, *percentages*

17 — Cameroon, CAR

21 — Congo, Zaire,

32 — Gabon

TEST-TUBE BABIES

Use of in-vitro fertilization, mid-1985	first practised	babies born number	centres number		first practised	babies born number	centres number
France	1978	100-200	over 60	Denmark	1982	1	2-3
	1979		70		1982-85		
USA	1980	about 180	about 108	Switzerland	1982-83	2	(quite) 7
	1982				1983		
Brazil	1982	2-3	6	Netherlands	1983	20	8

PUTTING MONEY WHERE THE MOUTH IS

Cents or fractions of a cent spent on family planning out of every dollar the central government spends, selected examples, most recent year since 1976

3.1
Bangladesh

| 0.8 | 0.48 | 0.4 | 0.13 | 0.06 | 0.04 |
| El Salvador | India | Mauritius | S. Korea | Singapore | Thaila |

| 0.59 | 0.44 | 0.3 | 0.09 | 0.05 | 0.02 |
| Pakistan | Philippines | Indonesia | Malaysia | Taiwan | Fiji |

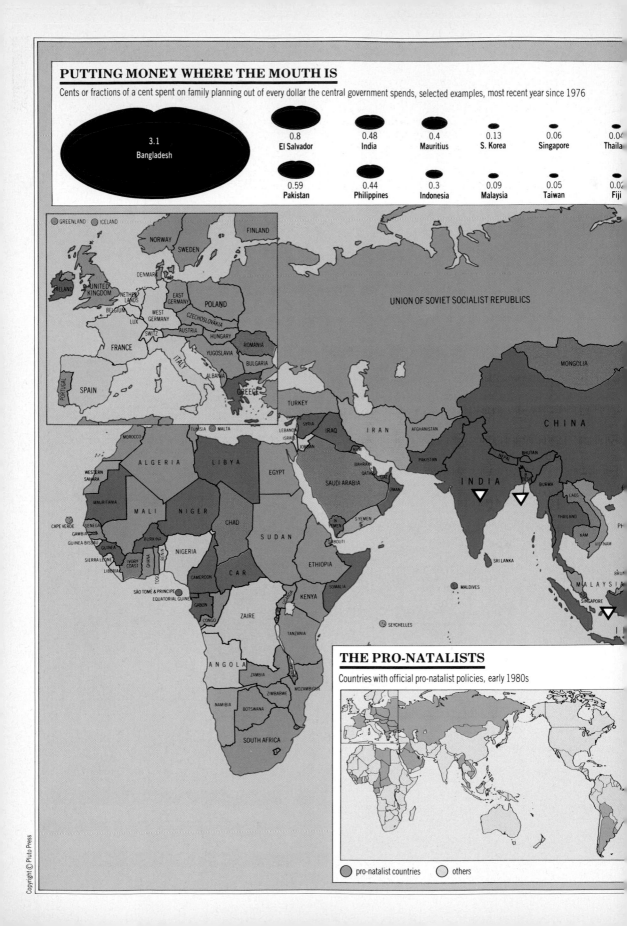

THE PRO-NATALISTS

Countries with official pro-natalist policies, early 1980s

● pro-natalist countries   ○ others

Most governments support some family planning: some subsidize contraceptive supplies, others give tax relief to smaller families. But everywhere, such resources fall far short of demand and millions of women have no family planning support. Funding commitments are a good indicator of actual government support.

Government involvement in family planning is not always beneficial. Some governments wield population-control policies with little regard for women's rights or health. Coercive sterilization, especially of poorer women and women from ethnic minority groups, is sometimes used to effect a quick reduction in population growth.

Pro-natalist governments want to increase population, often to ensure the continued supply of military manpower; this is sometimes accomplished by denying women family planning services.

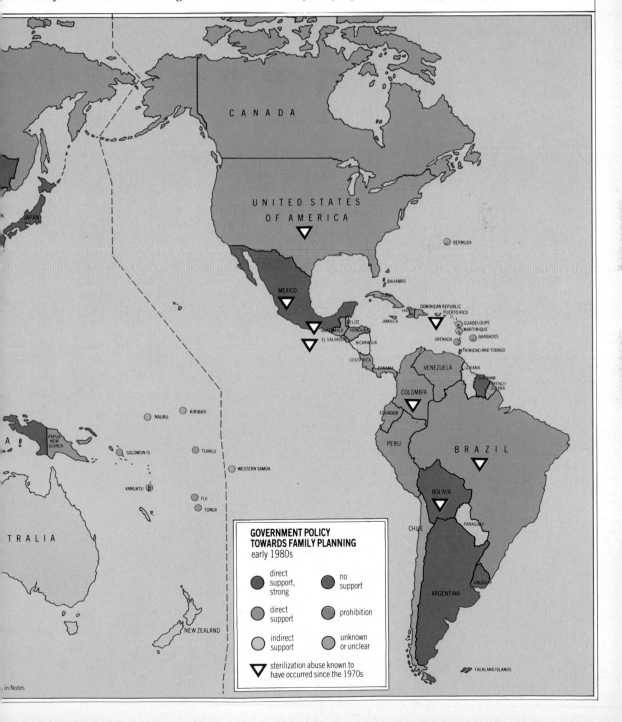

GOVERNMENT POLICY TOWARDS FAMILY PLANNING
early 1980s

- direct support, strong
- direct support
- indirect support
- no support
- prohibition
- unknown or unclear
- ▽ sterilization abuse known to have occurred since the 1970s

in Notes

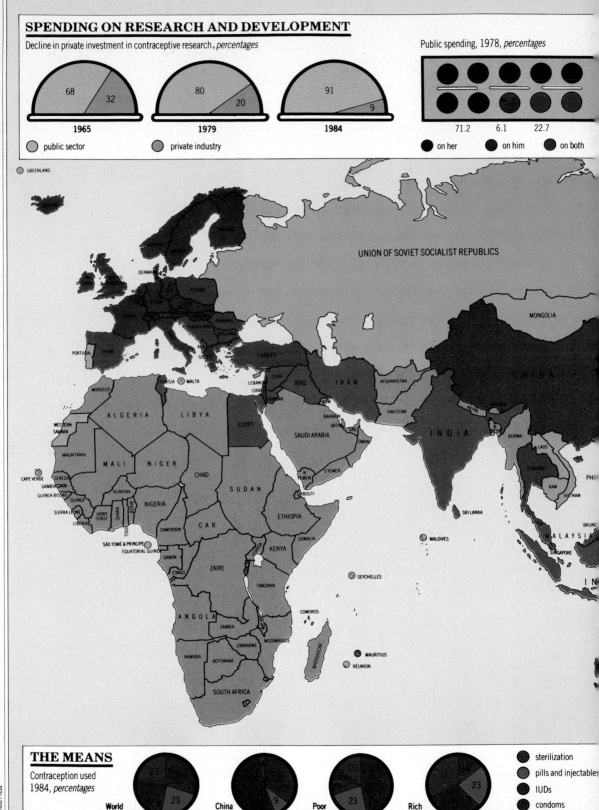

SPENDING ON RESEARCH AND DEVELOPMENT

Decline in private investment in contraceptive research, *percentages*

1965	1979	1984
68 / 32	80 / 20	91 / 9

- public sector
- private industry

Public spending, 1978, *percentages*

71.2   6.1   22.7

- on her
- on him
- on both

GREENLAND
ICELAND
NORWAY
SWEDEN
FINLAND
DENMARK
IRELAND
UNITED KINGDOM
NETHERLANDS
POLAND
GERMANY
FRANCE
CZECH
AUSTRIA
ROMANIA
YUGOSLAVIA
BULGARIA
ALB
GREECE
PORTUGAL
SPAIN
MALTA
TUNISIA
TURKEY
CYPRUS
LEBANON
SYRIA
ISRAEL
JORDAN
IRAQ
IRAN
AFGHANISTAN
PAKISTAN

UNION OF SOVIET SOCIALIST REPUBLICS

MONGOLIA
CHINA
NEPAL
BHUTAN
INDIA
BURMA
LAOS
THAILAND
KAM
VIETNAM
PHI

MOROCCO
WESTERN SAHARA
ALGERIA
LIBYA
EGYPT
SAUDI ARABIA
BAHRAIN
QATAR
UAE
OMAN
KUW
N YEMEN
S YEMEN
MAURITANIA
CAPE VERDE
SENEGAL
GAMBIA
GUINEA-BISSAU
GUINEA
SIERRA LEONE
LIBERIA
MALI
NIGER
CHAD
SUDAN
BURKINA
IVORY COAST
GHANA
BENIN
TOGO
NIGERIA
CAMEROON
CAR
ETHIOPIA
DJIBOUTI
SOMALIA
SÃO TOMÉ & PRINCIPE
EQUATORIAL GUINEA
GABON
CONGO
ZAIRE
UGANDA
KENYA
TANZANIA
SEYCHELLES
MALDIVES
SRI LANKA
MALAYSIA
SINGAPORE
BRUNE
IN

ANGOLA
ZAMBIA
ZIMBABWE
MOZAMBIQUE
COMOROS
NAMIBIA
BOTSWANA
MADAGASCAR
MAURITIUS
RÉUNION
SOUTH AFRICA

THE MEANS

Contraception used
1984, *percentages*

World except China
69 countries

China

Poor countries
50 countries

Rich countries
19 countries

- sterilization
- pills and injectables
- IUDs
- condoms
- traditional/other

Most women are expected to exercise some control over the number of children they bear. But what seems to be a personal choice of contraceptive methods is strongly influenced by many factors over which women have little control: national population policies (see 7. *Population Policies*), international contraceptive-aid policies, religious taboos, the dominant role of men in family decision-making, and the economics of the production and distribution of contraceptives. Wealthy women, women in wealthy countries, and urban women generally have the best access to contraceptive services.

Private industry has largely withdrawn from research into contraception in order to avoid legal liability for faulty or dangerous products. Research is now mostly paid for by governments.

Little research money goes into the development of male contraceptives.

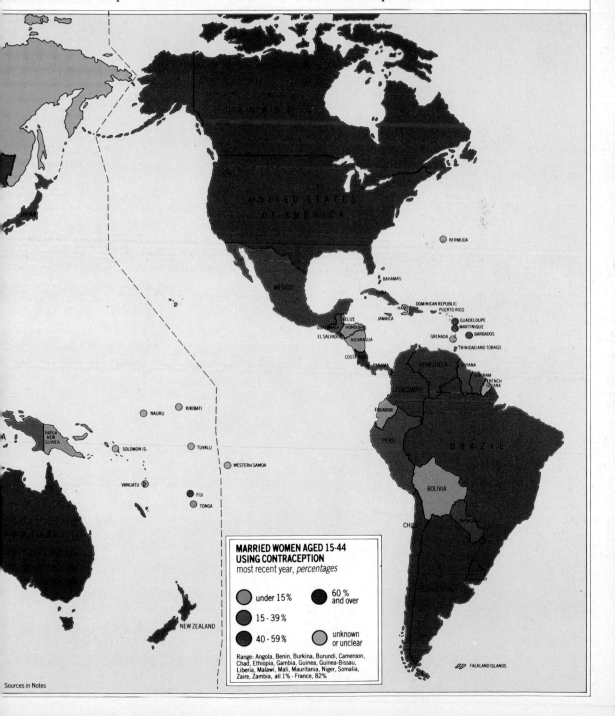

MARRIED WOMEN AGED 15-44 USING CONTRACEPTION
most recent year, *percentages*

- under 15%
- 15 - 39%
- 40 - 59%
- 60% and over
- unknown or unclear

Range: Angola, Benin, Burkina, Burundi, Cameroon, Chad, Ethiopia, Gambia, Guinea, Guinea-Bissau, Liberia, Malawi, Mali, Mauritania, Niger, Somalia, Zaire, Zambia, all 1% - France, 82%

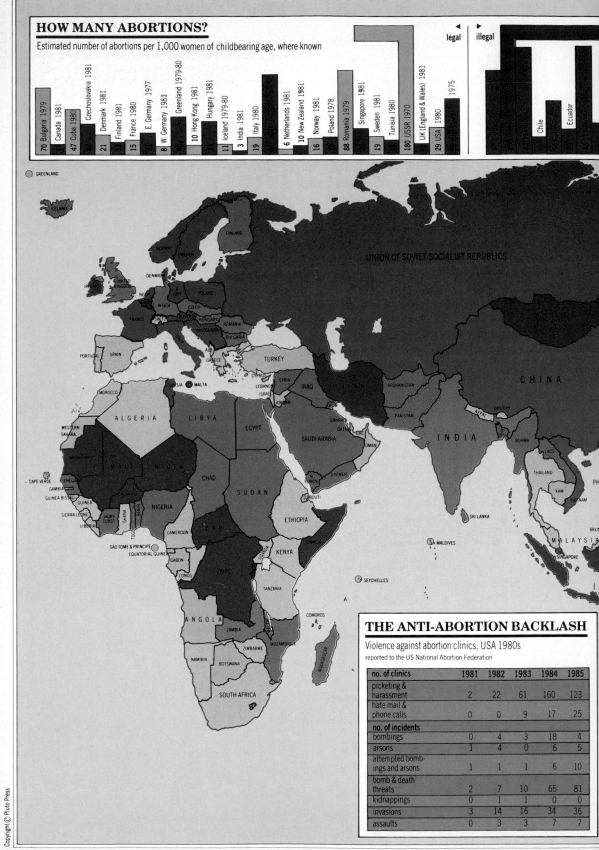

HOW MANY ABORTIONS?

Estimated number of abortions per 1,000 women of childbearing age, where known

◀ legal   ▶ illegal

70	Bulgaria 1979
	Canada 1981
47	Cuba 1980
	Czechoslovakia 1981
21	Denmark 1981
	Finland 1981
15	France 1980
	E. Germany 1977
8	W. Germany 1981
	Greenland 1979-80
10	Hong Kong 1981
	Hungary 1981
11	Iceland 1979-80
3	India 1981
19	Italy 1980
6	Netherlands 1981
10	New Zealand 1981
16	Norway 1981
	Poland 1978
88	Romania 1979
	Singapore 1981
19	Sweden 1981
	Tunisia 1980
180	USSR 1970
	UK (England & Wales) 1981
29	USA 1980
	1975
	Chile
	Ecuador

UNION OF SOVIET SOCIALIST REPUBLICS

GREENLAND
ICELAND
FINLAND
NORWAY
SWEDEN
DENMARK
UNITED KINGDOM
IRELAND
NETH
E GER
W GER
POLAND
FRANCE
SWITZ
AUSTRIA
CZECH
HUNGARY
ROMANIA
YUGOSLAVIA
BULGARIA
ITALY
ALB
GREECE
PORTUGAL
SPAIN
TURKEY
CYPRUS
TUNISIA
MALTA
SYRIA
LEBANON
ISRAEL
IRAQ
JORDAN
IRAN
AFGHANISTAN
CHINA
MOROCCO
WESTERN SAHARA
ALGERIA
LIBYA
EGYPT
SAUDI ARABIA
KUW
BAHRAIN
QATAR
UAE
OMAN
PAKISTAN
NEPAL
BHUTAN
INDIA
BURMA
CAPE VERDE
MAURITANIA
MALI
NIGER
CHAD
SUDAN
N YEMEN
S YEMEN
DJIBOUTI
ETHIOPIA
LAOS
THAILAND
KAM
VIETNAM
PHI
SENEGAL
GAMBIA
GUINEA BISSAU
GUINEA
SIERRA LEONE
LIBERIA
IVORY COAST
GHANA
TOGO
BENIN
BURKINA
NIGERIA
CAR
CAMEROON
SRI LANKA
MALDIVES
SÃO TOMÉ & PRINCIPE
EQUATORIAL GUINEA
GABON
CONGO
ZAIRE
UGANDA
KENYA
SOMALIA
MALAYSIA
SINGAPORE
BRUN
SEYCHELLES
TANZANIA
COMOROS
RWANDA
BURUNDI
ANGOLA
ZAMBIA
MALAWI
MOZAMBIQUE
MADAGASCAR
ZIMBABWE
NAMIBIA
BOTSWANA
SOUTH AFRICA

THE ANTI-ABORTION BACKLASH

Violence against abortion clinics, USA 1980s
reported to the US National Abortion Federation

no. of clinics	1981	1982	1983	1984	1985
picketing & harassment	2	22	61	160	123
hate mail & phone calls	0	0	9	17	25
no. of incidents					
bombings	0	4	3	18	4
arsons	1	4	0	6	5
attempted bombings and arsons	1	1	1	6	10
bomb & death threats	2	7	10	65	81
kidnappings	0	1	1	0	0
invasions	3	14	16	34	36
assaults	0	3	3	7	7

Abortion is an old and common form of birth control. The past two decades have seen a liberalizing trend in abortion laws.

Legal abortion gives women the right to control their own bodies, and helps them avoid the health risks of 'back-street' operations, giving poor women access to what rich women have always had. Abortion has also been used to promote government population policies.

But even in 'legal' countries, women often cannot afford, get access to, or get away with abortion. And in 'illegal' countries, abortions are still performed: by unskilled people under unclean conditions, resulting in death and disease among desperate women.

Opponents of abortion argue on religious, moral and even political grounds. Emotions run high where abortion is a matter of public debate, and the backlash has sometimes taken violent forms.

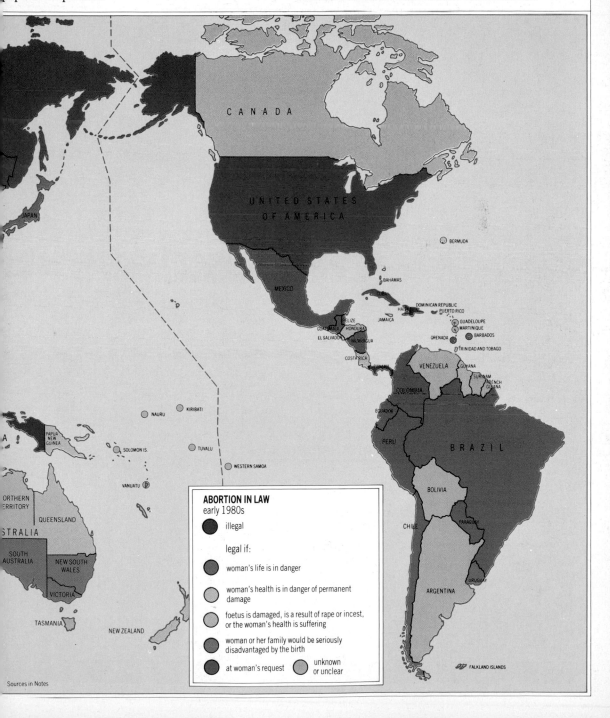

ABORTION IN LAW
early 1980s

- illegal

legal if:

- woman's life is in danger
- woman's health is in danger of permanent damage
- foetus is damaged, is a result of rape or incest, or the woman's health is suffering
- woman or her family would be seriously disadvantaged by the birth
- at woman's request
- unknown or unclear

Sources in Notes

INFANT MORTALITY IN A DIVIDED WORLD

Infant deaths per 1,000 live births, most recent year since 1979

● 101 and above   ● 51-100   ● 26-50   ○ 25 or under   ● unknown or unclear

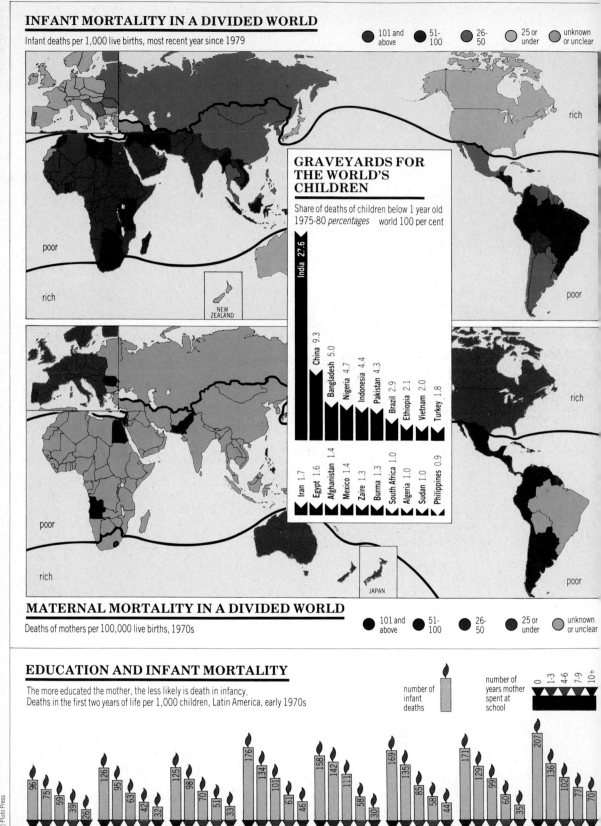

rich

poor

rich

NEW ZEALAND

poor

GRAVEYARDS FOR THE WORLD'S CHILDREN

Share of deaths of children below 1 year old
1975-80 *percentages*   world 100 per cent

India 27.6
China 9.3
Bangladesh 5.0
Nigeria 4.7
Indonesia 4.4
Pakistan 4.3
Brazil 2.9
Ethiopia 2.1
Vietnam 2.0
Turkey 1.8

Iran 1.7
Egypt 1.6
Afghanistan 1.4
Mexico 1.4
Zaire 1.3
Burma 1.3
South Africa 1.0
Algeria 1.0
Sudan 1.0
Philippines 0.9

rich

poor

poor

rich

JAPAN

MATERNAL MORTALITY IN A DIVIDED WORLD

Deaths of mothers per 100,000 live births, 1970s

● 101 and above   ● 51-100   ● 26-50   ● 25 or under   ○ unknown or unclear

EDUCATION AND INFANT MORTALITY

The more educated the mother, the less likely is death in infancy.
Deaths in the first two years of life per 1,000 children, Latin America, early 1970s

number of infant deaths

number of years mother spent at school   0 1-3 4-6 7-9 10+

Argentina 96 75 59 39 26
Colombia 126 95 63 42 32
Costa Rica 125 98 70 51 33
Ecuador 176 134 101 61 46
El Salvador 158 142 111 58 30
Guatemala 169 135 85 58 44
Honduras 171 129 99 60 35
Peru 207 136 102 77 70

Pregnancy and childbirth are major causes of death for women and children in all of the world's poorer countries. These countries constitute a recognized danger zone for childbearing women and their children. But even in the world's richest countries, maternal and infant mortality rates can be almost as high – for poor women and women from ethnic minorities. Everywhere, high death rates are associated with early marriage and childbearing (see 2. *Young Brides*), and with low levels of education for women.

The preference for boys throughout much of the world means that girls sometimes suffer severe neglect; this is reflected in patterns of child mortality. Girls are biologically stronger than boys at birth; in early infancy, their death rates are lower. But the balance shifts in early childhood, when death rates for girls surpass those for boys.

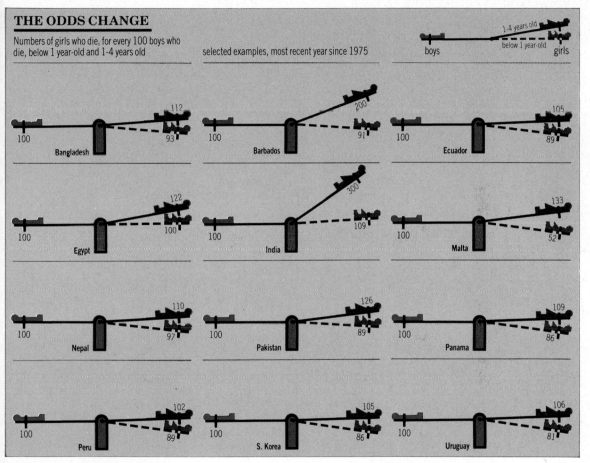

THE ODDS CHANGE

Numbers of girls who die, for every 100 boys who die, below 1 year-old and 1-4 years old

selected examples, most recent year since 1975

1-4 years old
below 1 year-old
boys   girls

Bangladesh: 100, 112, 93
Barbados: 100, 200, 91
Ecuador: 100, 105, 89
Egypt: 100, 122, 100
India: 100, 300, 109
Malta: 100, 133, 52
Nepal: 100, 110, 97
Pakistan: 100, 126, 89
Panama: 100, 109, 86
Peru: 100, 102, 89
S. Korea: 100, 105, 86
Uruguay: 100, 106, 81

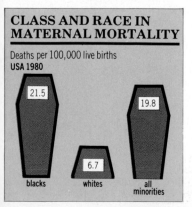

CLASS AND RACE IN MATERNAL MORTALITY

Deaths per 100,000 live births
USA 1980

- blacks: 21.5
- whites: 6.7
- all minorities: 19.8

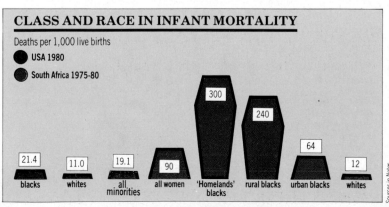

CLASS AND RACE IN INFANT MORTALITY

Deaths per 1,000 live births

- ● USA 1980
- ● South Africa 1975-80

- blacks: 21.4
- whites: 11.0
- all minorities: 19.1
- all women: 90
- 'Homelands' blacks: 300
- rural blacks: 240
- urban blacks: 64
- whites: 12

Sources in Notes

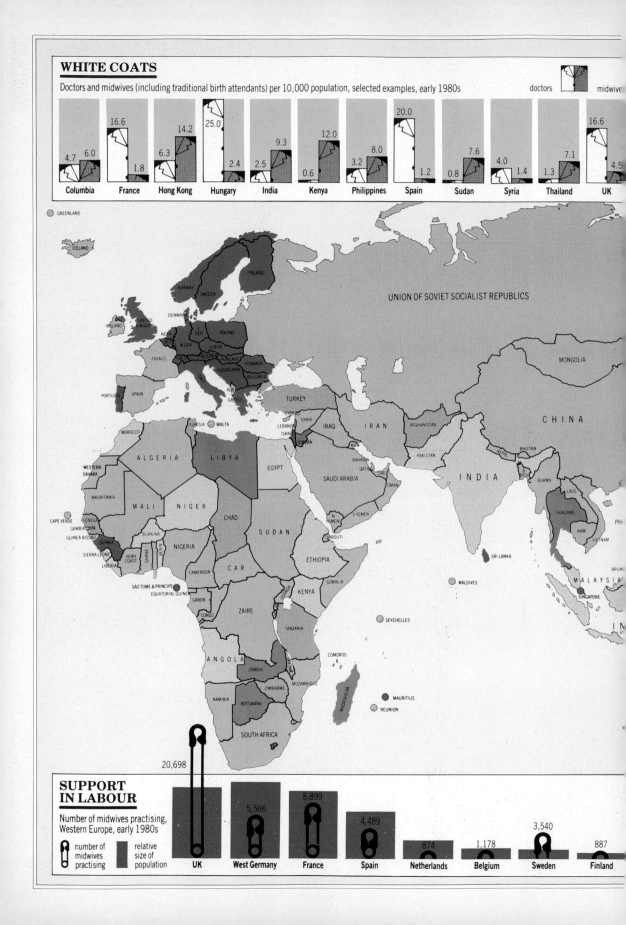

WHITE COATS

Doctors and midwives (including traditional birth attendants) per 10,000 population, selected examples, early 1980s

doctors ☐ midwives ■

	Columbia	France	Hong Kong	Hungary	India	Kenya	Philippines	Spain	Sudan	Syria	Thailand	UK
doctors	4.7	16.6	6.3	25.0	2.5	0.6	3.2	20.0	0.8	4.0	1.3	16.6
midwives	6.0	1.8	14.2	2.4	9.3	12.0	8.0	1.2	7.6	1.4	7.1	4.5

SUPPORT IN LABOUR

Number of midwives practising, Western Europe, early 1980s

☐ number of midwives practising

■ relative size of population

	UK	West Germany	France	Spain	Netherlands	Belgium	Sweden	Finland
	20,698	5,566	8,899	4,489	874	1,178	3,540	887

Midwives and traditional birth attendants deliver most of the world's babies. They are the primary source of health care and advice for most women during pregnancy, birth, and early childcare. 'Modern medicine' serves only a wealthier minority in the world, and is seldom available to rural women or the urban poor.

Until recently, most governments ignored or legislated against traditional birth attendants. Now, increasingly, they are being recognized as important primary health care providers, and they are being given medical training. But progress is slow, and the World Health Organization estimates that two-thirds of women in poor countries have no access to a trained health worker.

In rich countries, growing disenchantment with modern medicine's approach to birth care is leading to a resurgence of midwifery.

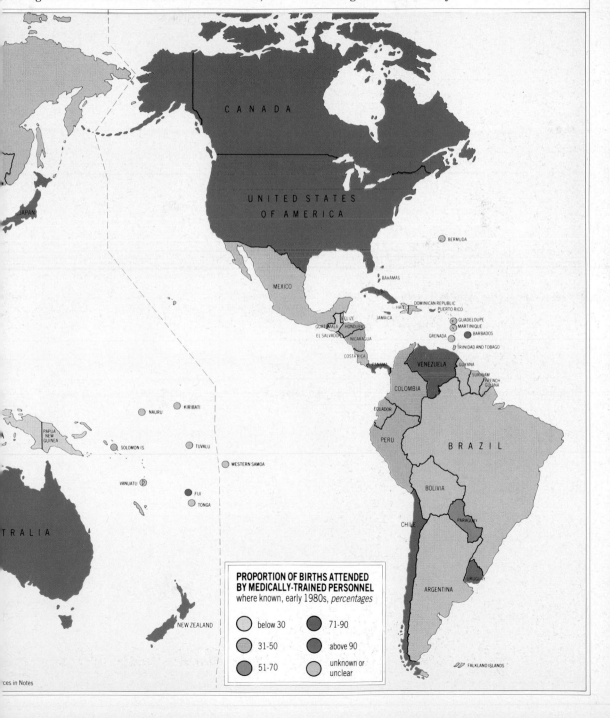

PROPORTION OF BIRTHS ATTENDED BY MEDICALLY-TRAINED PERSONNEL
where known, early 1980s, *percentages*

- below 30
- 31-50
- 51-70
- 71-90
- above 90
- unknown or unclear

HOMEWORK

The number of people per household, world, early 1980s, *percentages*

less than 3 | 3-3.9 | 4-4.9 | 5-5.9 | 6 or more

←——— **world population:** about 4,500 million ———→

| 12% | 9% | 41% | 36% |

46% of these in USA | 30% of these in Japan | 59% of these in China | 45% of these in India | 29% of the in Algeri

GREENLAND

ICELAND

NORWAY SWEDEN FINLAND

IRELAND UNITED KINGDOM DENMARK NETH BEL E GER POLAND W GER CZECH AUSTRIA HUNGARY ROMANIA FRANCE SWITZ YUGOSLAVIA BULGARIA ITALY PORTUGAL SPAIN GREECE

UNION OF SOVIET SOCIALIST REPUBLICS

MONGOLIA

TUNISIA MALTA

TURKEY

LEBANON SYRIA IRAQ IRAN AFGHANISTAN CHINA ISRAEL JORDAN KUWAIT PAKISTAN NEPAL BHUTAN

MOROCCO

WESTERN SAHARA ALGERIA LIBYA EGYPT SAUDI ARABIA QATAR U.A.E OMAN INDIA BURMA

MAURITANIA MALI NIGER CHAD SUDAN N YEMEN LAOS CAPE VERDE S YEMEN THAILAND SENEGAL GAMBIA BURKINA DJIBOUTI VIETNAM GUINEA-BISSAU GUINEA NIGERIA KAM SIERRA LEONE IVORY COAST GHANA ETHIOPIA SRI LANKA MALAYSIA LIBERIA TOGO BENIN CAR SÃO TOMÉ & PRÍNCIPE CAMEROON SOMALIA MALDIVES BRUNEI EQUATORIAL GUINEA GABON ZAIRE KENYA SINGAPORE CONGO

ANGOLA TANZANIA SEYCHELLES ZAMBIA COMOROS MALAWI NAMIBIA ZIMBABWE MOZAMBIQUE MADAGASCAR MAURITIUS BOTSWANA RÉUNION SOUTH AFRICA LESOTHO

CHILD CARE

Proportion of pre-school children in day care centres, latest year since 1978, *percentages*

 37 Sweden | 30 Norway | 25 China | 24 Bulgaria | 15 USA | 14 Canada | 8 Yugoslavia | 6 Kenya | 6 Tanzania | <1 Nicaragua | Botswan

Families and households are created and maintained almost entirely by women's labour. Many women, starting as young brides, spend their entire lives caring for them. There are a number of reasons, especially in poor countries, for having large families – they provide social security and a labour supply, for example. But families with many dependent children also place excessive demands on women's daily labour.

Worldwide, the nuclear family is replacing extended family living, and global trends are toward smaller families; but it is still true that one-third of the world's population live in households of five or more people.

Childcare accounts for the largest share of women's household labour – and limits their ability to take paid work outside the home. In only a few countries are there alternative childcare facilities.

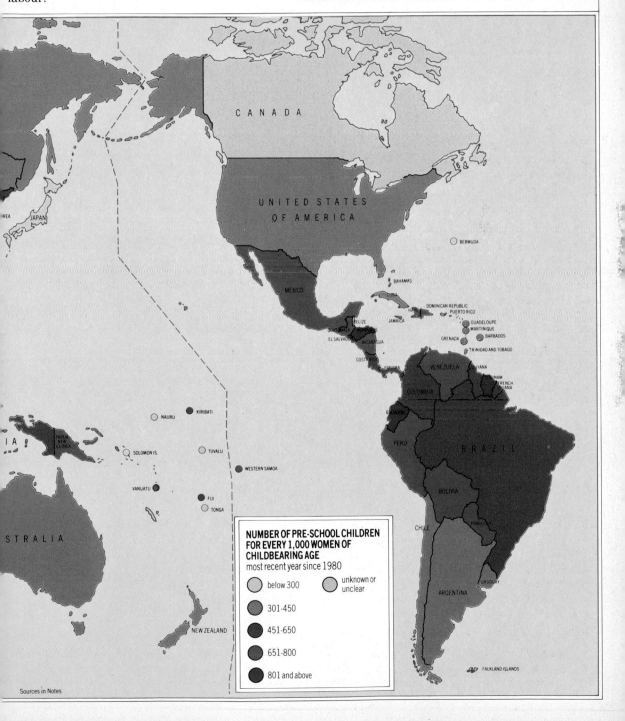

NUMBER OF PRE-SCHOOL CHILDREN FOR EVERY 1,000 WOMEN OF CHILDBEARING AGE
most recent year since 1980

- below 300
- unknown or unclear
- 301–450
- 451–650
- 651–800
- 801 and above

WOMEN'S WORK, MEN'S WORK

Proportion of certain types of work done by women and men, Africa, mid-1970s

♀ women ♂ men

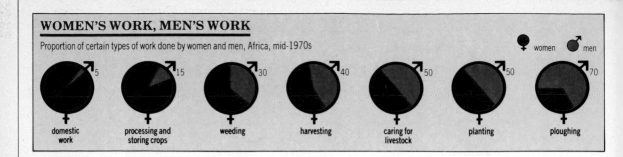

domestic work	processing and storing crops	weeding	harvesting	caring for livestock	planting	ploughing
5	15	30	40	50	50	70

UNSYNCHRONIZED CLOCKS

The number of hours spent by men for every 100 hours spent by women on certain activities, most recent year 1970s and 1980s

women   men

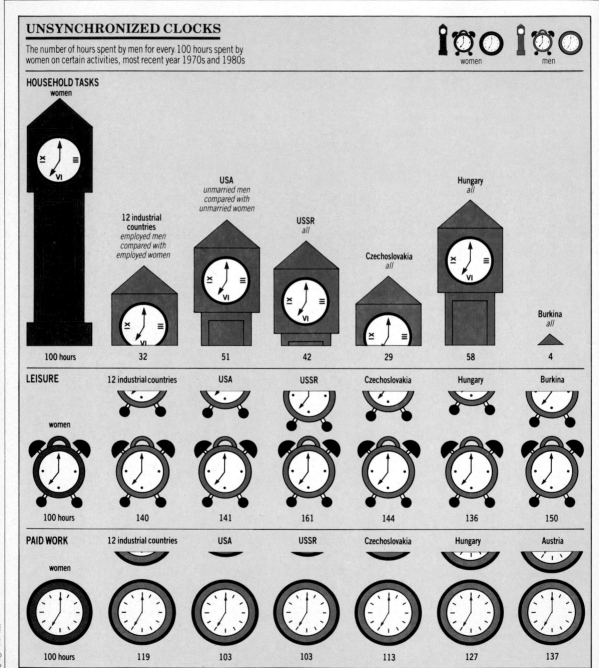

HOUSEHOLD TASKS

women

12 industrial countries
employed men compared with employed women

USA
unmarried men compared with unmarried women

USSR
all

Czechoslovakia
all

Hungary
all

Burkina
all

| 100 hours | 32 | 51 | 42 | 29 | 58 | 4 |

LEISURE

women

	12 industrial countries	USA	USSR	Czechoslovakia	Hungary	Burkina
100 hours	140	141	161	144	136	150

PAID WORK

women

	12 industrial countries	USA	USSR	Czechoslovakia	Hungary	Austria
100 hours	119	103	103	113	127	137

TIME BUDGETS

Women work longer hours than men do. Women do the household chores and take care of the children. They tend the goats, till the family garden, collect water, gather firewood.

Women are also entering the paid workforce in increasing numbers, but no one is taking over at home. Busy, fatigued mothers cannot pursue training or education that might help develop their self-sufficiency or alleviate drudgery. Only one side of the traditional division of labour is breaking down and only three countries in the world have made the sharing of housework official public policy.

Women everywhere get little financial or social recognition for working more, resting less, and doing a greater variety of work than men. Their work is often statistically invisible: it is estimated that the official enumerators count only about two-thirds of women's work.

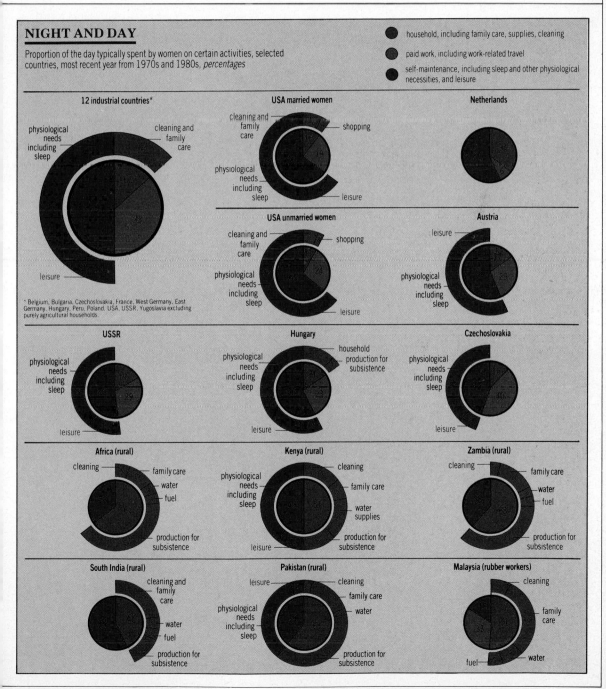

NIGHT AND DAY

Proportion of the day typically spent by women on certain activities, selected countries, most recent year from 1970s and 1980s, *percentages*

- household, including family care, supplies, cleaning
- paid work, including work-related travel
- self-maintenance, including sleep and other physiological necessities, and leisure

Sources in Notes

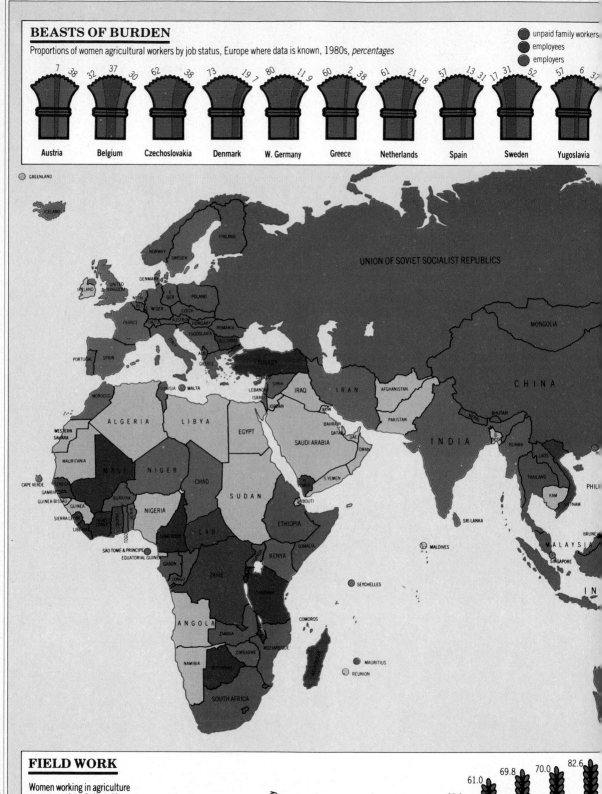

BEASTS OF BURDEN

Proportions of women agricultural workers by job status, Europe where data is known, 1980s, *percentages*

- unpaid family workers
- employees
- employers

7 38	32 37 30	62 38	73 19 7	80 11 9	60 2 38	61 21 18	57 13 31	17 31 52	57 6 37
Austria	Belgium	Czechoslovakia	Denmark	W. Germany	Greece	Netherlands	Spain	Sweden	Yugoslavia

FIELD WORK

Women working in agriculture as a proportion of all working women, countries with over 50 million population, most recent year from 1975, *percentages*

Mexico	USA	UK	West Germany	France	Italy	Brazil	Japan	Philippines	Indonesia	Bangladesh	Pakistan	India
0.3	0.4	1.0	5.0	8.0	14.0	17.0	18.0	28.2	61.0	69.8	70.0	82.6

Women produce at least half the world's output of food, mostly in poor, agricultural countries where they grow, harvest and prepare virtually all the food consumed by their families. In Africa they perform 60 to 80 per cent of agricultural work.

In Asia and Africa, almost all women who are employed work in agriculture: in Mozambique, for example, 90 per cent of working women are engaged in the production of food.

Because much of women's agricultural work is done in or near the home, is small in scale, part-time or seasonal, it is considered unimportant by official agencies. As a result, women are often left out of economic development schemes.

Women are at the bottom of the pay and power scales in agriculture: they are employees, not employers; unpaid sowers, reapers and breadmakers; not breadwinners on the human 'family farm'.

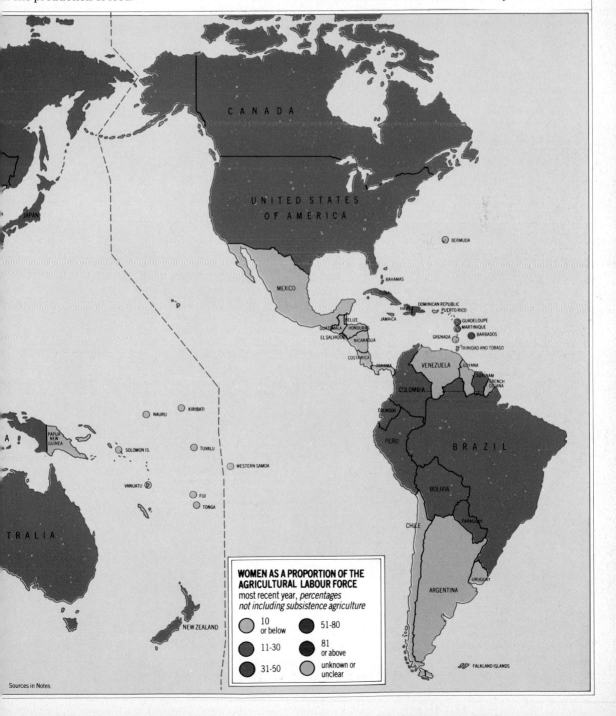

WOMEN AS A PROPORTION OF THE AGRICULTURAL LABOUR FORCE
most recent year, *percentages*
not including subsistence agriculture

- 10 or below
- 11-30
- 31-50
- 51-80
- 81 or above
- unknown or unclear

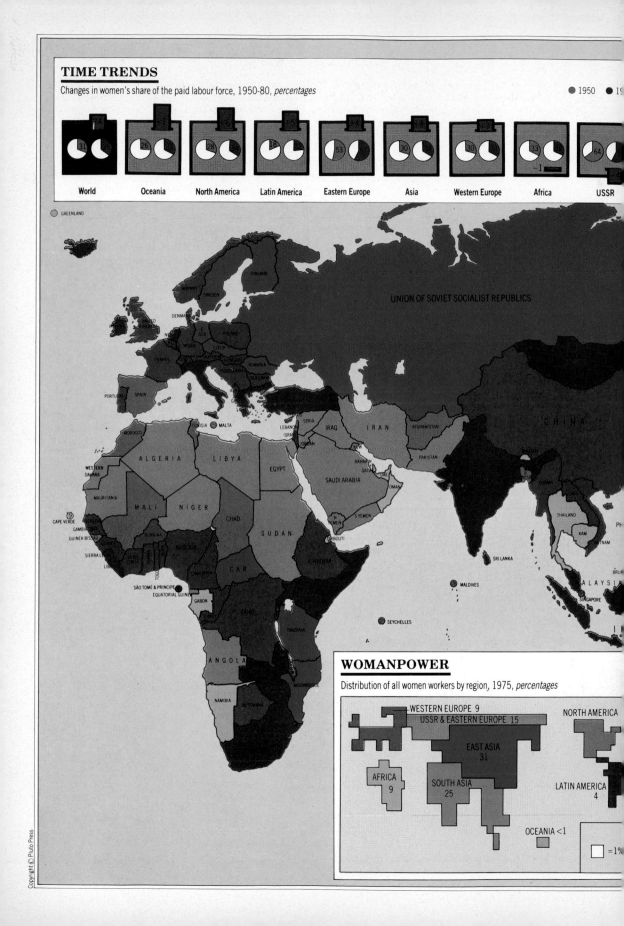

TIME TRENDS

Changes in women's share of the paid labour force, 1950-80, *percentages*

● 1950 ● 19

World	Oceania	North America	Latin America	Eastern Europe	Asia	Western Europe	Africa	USSR

GREENLAND

FINLAND

NORWAY SWEDEN

DENMARK

UNITED KINGDOM

UNION OF SOVIET SOCIALIST REPUBLICS

E GER POLAND

CZECH

FRANCE AUSTRIA HUNGARY ROMANIA

BULGARIA

PORTUGAL SPAIN

TUNISIA MALTA

SYRIA

LEBANON IRAQ I R A N AFGHANISTAN

ISRAEL

JORDAN

C H I N A

MOROCCO

KUW

WESTERN
SAHARA

BAHRAIN

PAKISTAN

A L G E R I A L I B Y A EGYPT QATAR UAE

SAUDI ARABIA OMAN

MAURITANIA

BURMA

M A L I N I G E R

THAILAND

CAPE VERDE CHAD

GAMBIA S YEMEN KAM PH

GUINEA BISSAU BURKINA N YEMEN VITNAM

SIERRA LE NIGERIA S U D A N DJIBOUTI

LIB

TOGO ETHIOPIA SRI LANKA BRU

SÃO TOMÉ & PRINCIPE C A R MALDIVES M A L A Y S I A

EQUATORIAL GUINEA CAMEROON

GABON SINGAPORE

SEYCHELLES

A N G O L A

TANZANIA

MOZAMBIQUE

NAMIBIA BOTSWANA

WOMANPOWER

Distribution of all women workers by region, 1975, *percentages*

WESTERN EUROPE 9	NORTH AMERICA
USSR & EASTERN EUROPE 15	
EAST ASIA 31	
AFRICA 9	SOUTH ASIA 25	LATIN AMERICA 4

OCEANIA <1

□ =1%

Women represent about one-third of the paid labour force worldwide. This share is slowly growing in most places, with the largest increases occurring in industrializing countries. In two regions, women's labour force rates appear to have decreased over the past thirty years.

The picture of women's work that can be drawn from official labour force statistics, however, is unreliable and incomplete. It is widely understood that more women are working for wages, and at a greater rate of increase, than is revealed by these numbers. Increasingly, when women enter waged work, they do so 'in the 'informal' sector, as domestic servants and market traders, for example – labour that is often uncounted.

Several countries with unusually high records of women in the paid work force are also those with high rates of male emigration.

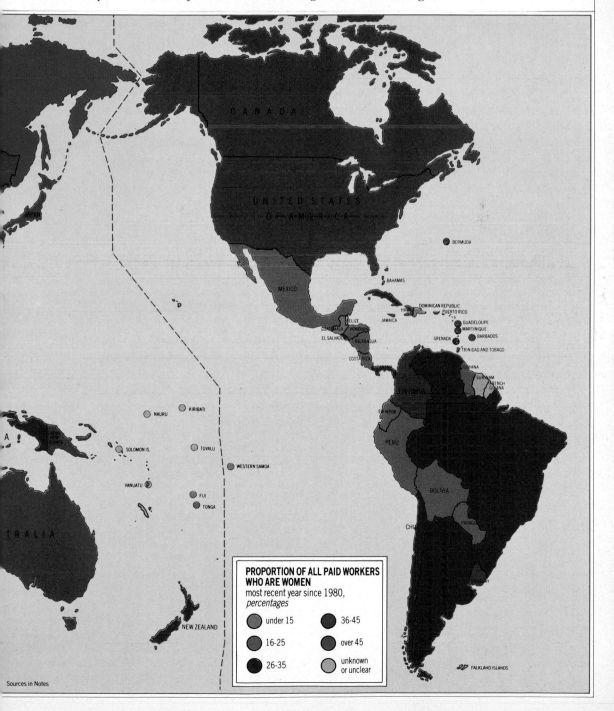

PROPORTION OF ALL PAID WORKERS WHO ARE WOMEN
most recent year since 1980, *percentages*

- under 15
- 16-25
- 26-35
- 36-45
- over 45
- unknown or unclear

Sources in Notes

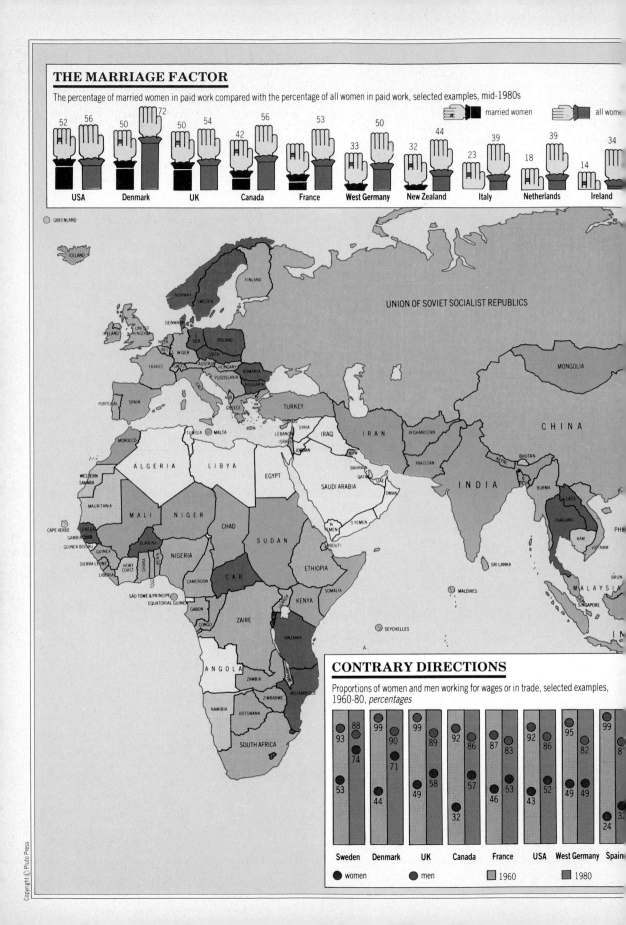

THE MARRIAGE FACTOR

The percentage of married women in paid work compared with the percentage of all women in paid work, selected examples, mid-1980s

married women   all wome[n]

52	56	50	72	50	54	42	56	53	50	33	32	44	23	39	18	39	14	34

USA   Denmark   UK   Canada   France   West Germany   New Zealand   Italy   Netherlands   Ireland

GREENLAND

ICELAND

NORWAY SWEDEN FINLAND

UNION OF SOVIET SOCIALIST REPUBLICS

DENMARK
IRELAND
UNITED KINGDOM
NETH
BEL
E GER
W GER POLAND
CZECH
FRANCE SWITZ AUSTRIA HUNGARY
YUGOSLAVIA ROMANIA
ITALY BULGARIA
ALB
PORTUGAL SPAIN GREECE
TURKEY
CYPRUS SYRIA
TUNISIA MALTA LEBANON IRAQ I R A N AFGHANISTAN
ISRAEL
JORDAN
MOROCCO
MONGOLIA
C H I N A
BHUTAN
KUW PAKISTAN NEPAL
WESTERN
SAHARA A L G E R I A L I B Y A EGYPT BAHRAIN
QATAR I N D I A BURMA
UAE
MAURITANIA OMAN LAOS
M A L I N I G E R CHAD SAUDI ARABIA THAILAND
CAPE VERDE N
SENEGAL YEMEN S YEMEN KAM PH
GAMBIA BURKINA SUDAN DJIBOUTI VIETNAM
GUINEA BISSAU NIGERIA SRI LANKA
GUINEA BENIN BRUN
SIERRA LEONE IVORY GHANA C A R ETHIOPIA MALDIVES M A L A Y S I A
LIBERIA COAST TOGO CAMEROON
SÃO TOMÉ & PRINCIPE SOMALIA SINGAPORE
EQUATORIAL GUINEA KENYA
GABON
CONGO Z A I R E SEYCHELLES I[N]
TANZANIA

A N G O L A
ZAMBIA
ZIMBABWE MOZAMBIQUE
NAMIBIA BOTSWANA

SOUTH AFRICA

CONTRARY DIRECTIONS

Proportions of women and men working for wages or in trade, selected examples, 1960-80, *percentages*

	Sweden	Denmark	UK	Canada	France	USA	West Germany	Spain
men 1960	93	99	99	92	87	92	95	99
men 1980	88	90	89	86	83	86	82	8[ ]
women 1960	53	44	49	49	46	43	49	24
women 1980	74	71	58	57	53	52	49	3[ ] / 32

● women   ● men   1960   1980

ost women who work outside the home do so be-
ause they have to – this is true whether the work is
ading beans in a market, or typing in an office.
omen's wages, increasingly, are essential for fami-
 survival. At the same time, women have primary
esponsibility for maintaining their families and
ouseholds – work outside must be fitted around
omestic duties. For many women, this means work-
g a double day.

The proportion of women who work outside the
home varies widely from country to country.
Although more women are now working, in almost
all cultures, there is resistance to it. This is especially
true with regard to married women; men commonly
feel it a dishonour for their wives to work. Employers
often will not hire married women.

The strongest constraints on women being active
outside the home exist in Islamic countries.

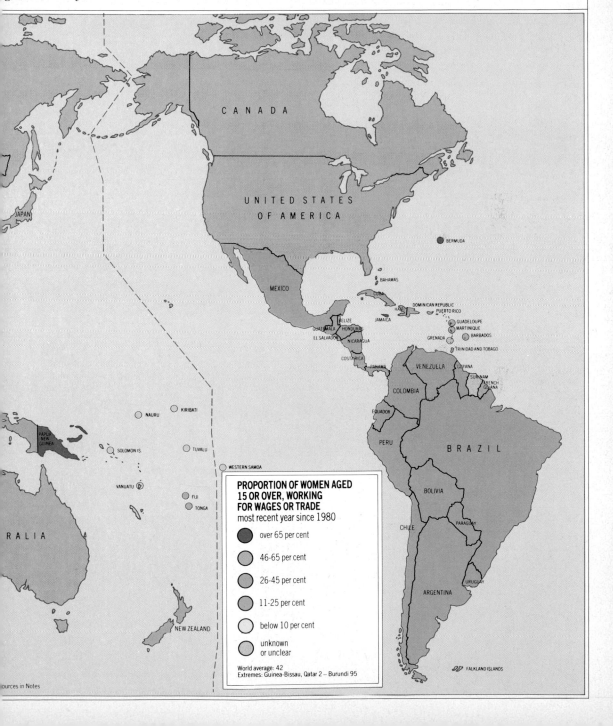

**PROPORTION OF WOMEN AGED
15 OR OVER, WORKING
FOR WAGES OR TRADE**
most recent year since 1980

over 65 per cent

46-65 per cent

26-45 per cent

11-25 per cent

below 10 per cent

unknown
or unclear

World average: 42
Extremes: Guinea-Bissau, Qatar 2 – Burundi 95

MEN ON THE MOVE

Countries where migration for work is predominantly male, 1980s

| Botswana | Egypt | Lesotho | Mozambique | Sudan | Vietnam |

GREENLAND   ICELAND

NORWAY
SWEDEN
FINLAND

DENMARK

IRELAND
UNITED
KINGDOM

NETHER-
LANDS
BELGIUM
EAST
GERMANY
POLAND

WEST
GERMANY
LUX
CZECHOSLOVAKIA
HUNGARY
ROMANIA

FRANCE

YUGOSLAVIA
BULGARIA

ALBANIA

GREECE

UNION OF SOVIET SOCIALIST REPUBLICS

MONGOLIA

CHINA

PORTUGAL
SPAIN
ITALY

WESTERN
SAHARA
MAURITANIA
MALI
NIGER

ALGERIA
LIBYA
EGYPT

TUNISIA   MALTA
CYPRUS
LEBANON
ISRAEL

SAUDI ARABIA
BAHRAIN

OMAN

PAKISTAN
NEPAL
BHUTAN

INDIA
BURMA

① Italy to Switzerland
② Italy to West Germany
③ Yugoslavia to West Germany
④ Yugoslavia to Switzerland
⑤ Spain to West Germany
⑥ Yugoslavia to Austria/Switzerland

Portugal to France

Spain to France/West Germany

Morocco to France

Algeria to France

Tunisia to France

Turkey to West Germany

Turkey to Netherlands/Austria/Sweden

India Bangladesh Pakistan Sri Lanka Malaysia to Western Europe

Sri Lanka to Middle East

Thailand to Western Europe

FROM COUNTRY TO TOWN

Internal migration for work, 1980s

● men and women   ● predominantly wo[men]

rich

poor

rich

poor

here is a huge rural to urban migration currently nderway throughout the Third World. In some laces, it is mostly the men who move to cities for ork – sometimes never returning, and leaving in neir wake a large population of poor, women-eaded families (see 28. *Poverty*). In Latin America nd parts of Asia, women outnumber men in the earch for a new life and work in the cities.

Women also make up a large proportion of inter-national migrants, as part of families or on their own. Some migrant streams are created by em-ployers or governments recruiting 'cheap labour', such as the thousands of women brought from Sri Lanka to be domestic servants in the Middle East.

For many women, their new life is no better than the one they left behind, and may be worse. Migrant women are among the poorest of the poor, triply burdened by race, class and gender barriers.

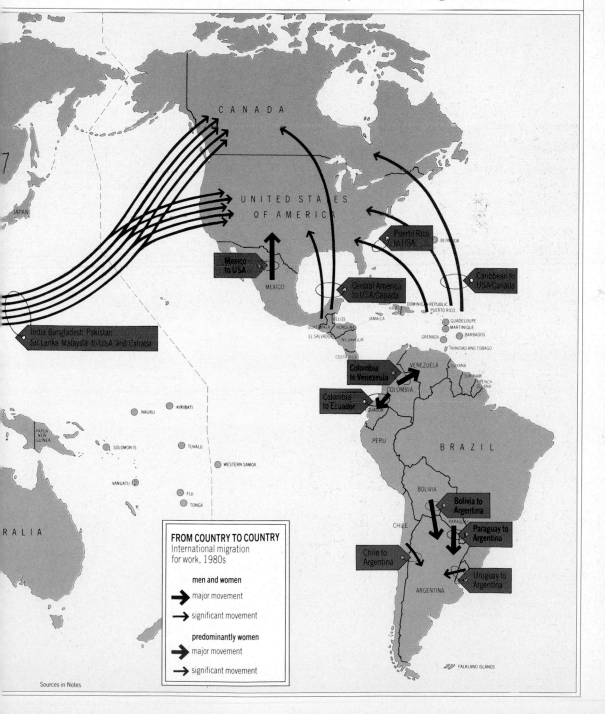

FROM COUNTRY TO COUNTRY
International migration
for work, 1980s

men and women
→ major movement
→ significant movement

predominantly women
→ major movement
→ significant movement

Sources in Notes

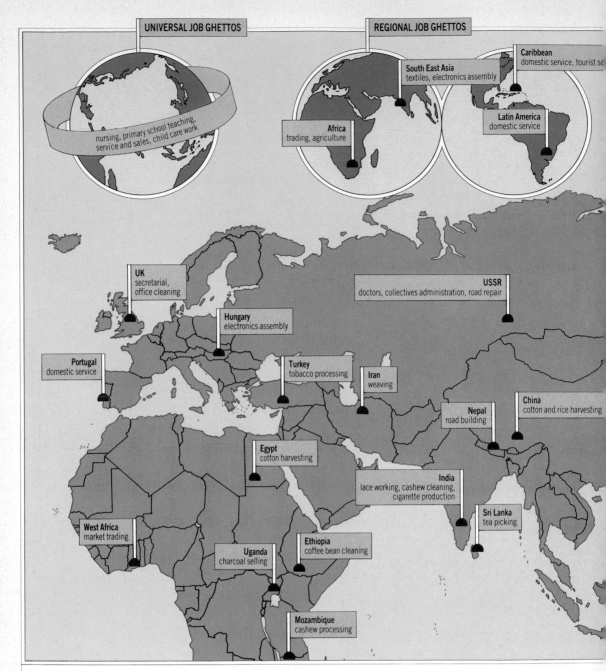

nursing, primary school teaching, service and sales, child care work

South East Asia
textiles, electronics assembly

Caribbean
domestic service, tourist se

Africa
trading, agriculture

Latin America
domestic service

UK
secretarial,
office cleaning

USSR
doctors, collectives administration, road repair

Portugal
domestic service

Hungary
electronics assembly

Turkey
tobacco processing

Iran
weaving

China
cotton and rice harvesting

Nepal
road building

Egypt
cotton harvesting

India
lace working, cashew cleaning,
cigarette production

Sri Lanka
tea picking

West Africa
market trading

Uganda
charcoal selling

Ethiopia
coffee bean cleaning

Mozambique
cashew processing

THREE JOB AREAS

Women as a proportion of waged
workers, early 1980s, *percentages*

- 15 and below
- 46-60
- 16-30
- over 60
- 31-45
- unknown or unclear

1 Administration and management

2 Clerical work

3 Manufacturing

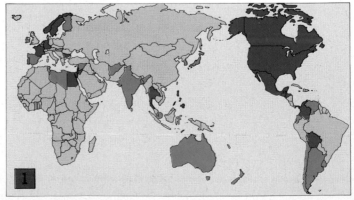

The range of jobs that women fill in the workforce is much narrower than for men. And, in every country and every region of the world, there are jobs that are specifically defined as 'women's work'. These are the jobs that are filled almost exclusively by women – and are usually considered beneath men's station.

In some countries, almost all bank tellers and secretaries are women. In other countries, tea picking and cotton harvesting are considered women's work. In Latin America and the Caribbean, domestic service is almost entirely feminized, and up to 80 per cent of all women who earn wages work as servants. In South East Asia, textile manufacturing and electronics assembly rely heavily on female labour – and, especially, on a young, female workforce.

Although specifics vary, it is universally true that jobs defined as women's work carry low pay, low status, and little security: thus termed, 'job ghettos'.

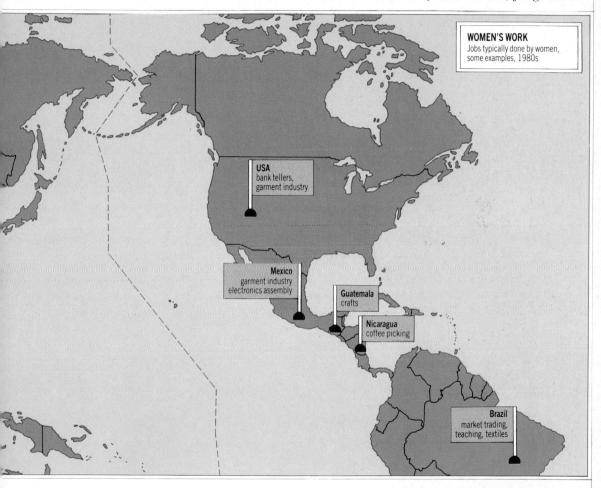

WOMEN'S WORK
Jobs typically done by women, some examples, 1980s

USA
bank tellers, garment industry

Mexico
garment industry electronics assembly

Guatemala
crafts

Nicaragua
coffee picking

Brazil
market trading, teaching, textiles

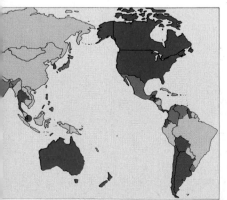

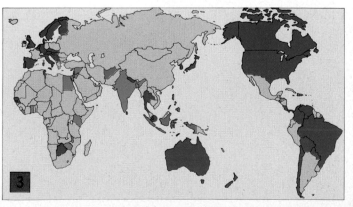

3

WOMEN EARN LESS THAN MEN IN THE SAME JOB CATEGORY

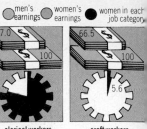
men's earnings | women's earnings | women in each job category

Women's earnings as a percentage of men's earnings, selected job categories, USA, 1981

Percentage of women workers in each job category, USA, 1981

64.7 / 100
all occupations

71.8 / 100
professional and technical

60.8 / 100
managers and administrators

52.0 / 100
sales workers

67.0 / 100
clerical workers

66.5 / 100
5.6
craft workers

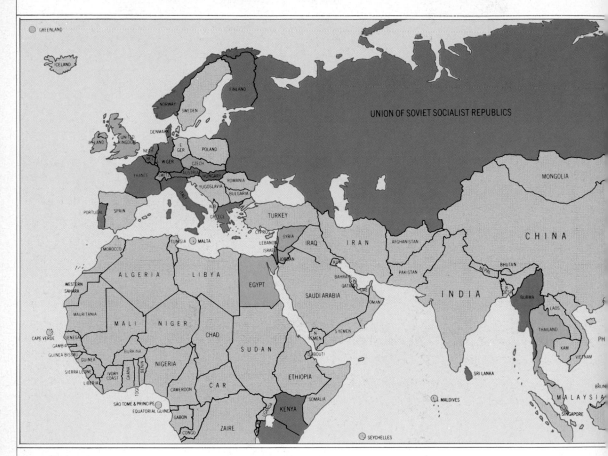

PART TIME WORKERS

women
men

Proportion of all women and men at work who work part-time, where data is known, most recent year since 1980, *percentages*

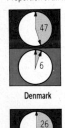
47 / 6
Denmark

45 / <1
Norway

44 / 5
Sweden

44 / 3
UK

36 / 5
Switzerland

35 / 5
Australia

33 / 2
Ireland

33 / 18
USA

29 / 2

West Germany

26 / 5
New Zealand

24 / 6
Canada

19 / 10
Netherlands

18 / 2
Austria

17 / 2
France

17 / 2
Portugal

16 / 1
Belgium

12 / 3
Finland

10 / 3

Italy

Women are ghettoized in low-paying jobs (see 18. *Job Ghettos*), are often denied promotions, and commonly face outright wage discrimination. They have little job protection (see 20. *Job Protection*), and form the bulk of part-time workers. As a result, women everywhere earn less than men. This is true even when they do the same work as men, and true even in occupations where women form the majority of workers (such as clerical work).

The earnings gap is universal and growing – in spite of equal pay laws which exist in a great number of countries. Such laws are not often enforced, nor do they generally apply to part-time workers or workers in the informal sector, where women predominate. Wage legislation by itself does not remove the inequalities that create the gap in the first place.

Women's relative underpayment in work is a major factor in the growing feminization of poverty.

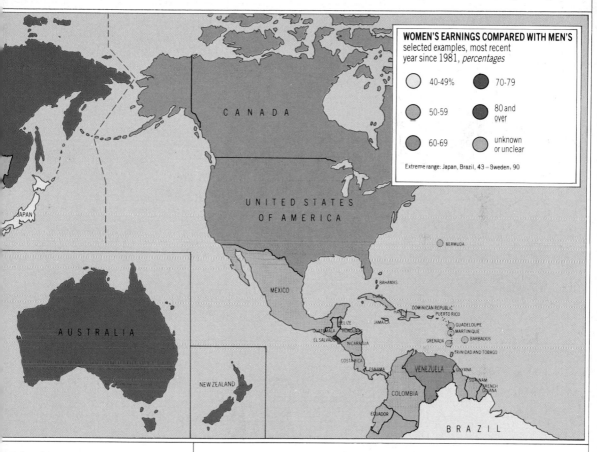

WOMEN'S EARNINGS COMPARED WITH MEN'S
selected examples, most recent year since 1981, *percentages*

- 40-49%
- 50-59
- 60-69
- 70-79
- 80 and over
- unknown or unclear

Extreme range: Japan, Brazil, 43 – Sweden, 90

SOME WOMEN EARN EVEN LESS

Women's earnings as a percentage of white men's earnings, early 1980s

USA

- white women 66
- black women 60
- Hispanic women 55
- white men 100

Black women's earnings as a percentage of white and black men's earnings, early 1980s

South Africa

- black women 8
- white men 100
- black women 60
- black men 100

IN THE EYES OF THE LAW

National laws and international conventions of equal pay, 1985

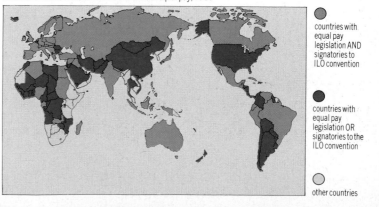

- countries with equal pay legislation AND signatories to ILO convention
- countries with equal pay legislation OR signatories to the ILO convention
- other countries

TAKING THE STRAIN

Women's share of the increase in unemployment 1976-80, selected rich countries, *percentages*

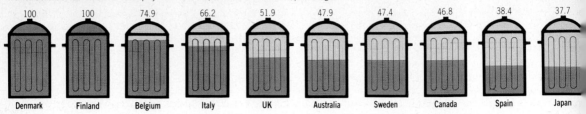

100	100	74.9	66.2	51.9	47.9	47.4	46.8	38.4	37.7
Denmark	Finland	Belgium	Italy	UK	Australia	Sweden	Canada	Spain	Japan

A WORKER'S RIGHT TO MOTHERHOOD: A MOTHER'S RIGHT TO WORK

States with national legislation providing for maternity leave and pay, 1980s

- maternity leave of 12 weeks or more on full pay (ILO standard)
- maternity leave of 12 weeks or more without full pay
- maternity leave of less than 12 weeks but with full pay
- some leave and pay provisions, but below ILO standard
- no provision, unknown or unclear
- ✓ job tenure a legal provision for pregnant workers

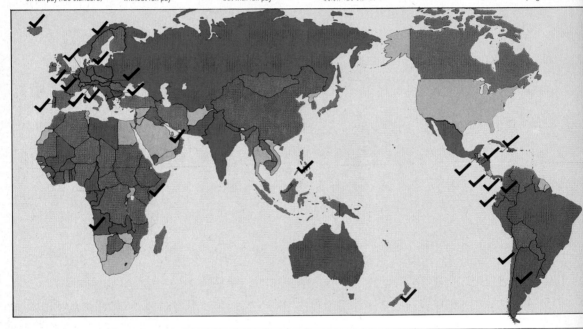

UNREPRESENTATIVES

Women as a proportion of trade union officials, selected countries, selected examples, 1980s, *percentages*

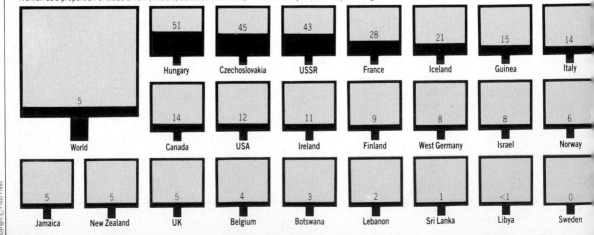

5	51	45	43	28	21	15	14
World	Hungary	Czechoslovakia	USSR	France	Iceland	Guinea	Italy

14	12	11	9	8	8	6
Canada	USA	Ireland	Finland	West Germany	Israel	Norway

5	5	5	4	3	2	1	<1	0
Jamaica	New Zealand	UK	Belgium	Botswana	Lebanon	Sri Lanka	Libya	Sweden

As more women become employed in the formal economy, more of them also become unemployed – at a rate that is rising faster then the rate for men. Women's unemployment is considered to be a less serious problem than men's, but in many countries recent increases in unemployment have been borne almost entirely by women. It is not unusual to find that women's share of registered unemployment is greater than their share of employment.

Many women lose their jobs in trying to balance the conflicting demands that come from having to be both mothers and waged workers. While expected to perform both roles fully and effectively, women receive little support to do so. Maternity policies in most countries leave women with no job protection. And ´unions generally do not take up issues of women's rights, partly because there are few women in policy-making positions within them.

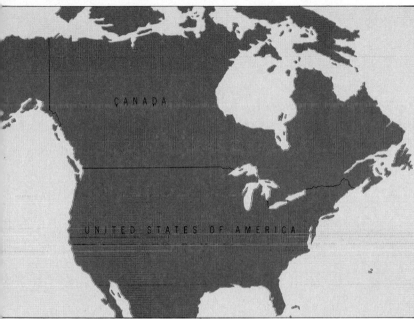

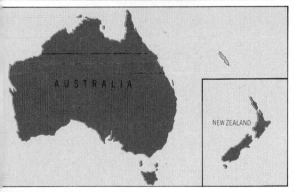

WOMEN'S SHARE OF UNEMPLOYMENT AND EMPLOYMENT COMPARED

rich countries, most recent year since 1982

● share of unemployment greater than share of employment

● share of unemployment more or less equal to share of employment

● share of unemployment less than share of employment

extremes: Portugal, share of unemployment 30 percentage points more than share of employment – UK, share of unemployment 12 percentage points less than share of employment.

INHERITANCE RIGHTS

Countries where women (or some women, living under customary or religious laws) do not have the same rights as men to inherit wealth or property, where known, 1980s

● women do not have the same rights as men   ● unknown, unclea and others

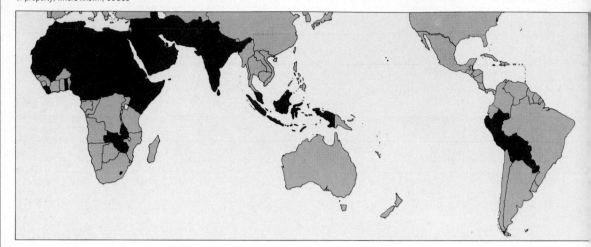

HOME RULE

Countries where the choice of domicile for a married couple is the husband's by law, and the wife is obliged to follow, where known, 1980s

● women do not have the same rights as men   ● unknown, unclea and others

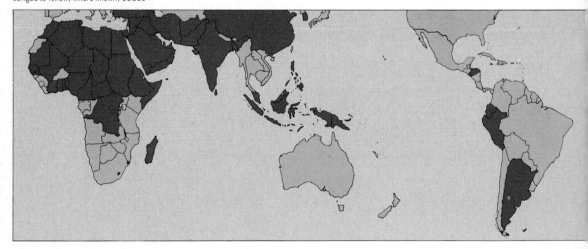

MANAGING MONEY

Women in finance, insurance and real estate, where known, 1980s, *percentages*

● women as a proportion of all worker

Sweden	Japan	West Germany	Norway	Venezuela	Hungary
47.2	43.0	47.8	45.3	37.8	48.2
1.2	0.7	1.4	4.3	2.7	0.0

In much of the world, property is the key to survival and women do not have the same rights to property as men. Where women do not share equal rights in marriage, they do not have equal access to property. Where property is held jointly it is almost everywhere controlled by the husband. And amongst the many without property in the world, women are the most destitute.

The ownership of land is a particularly important case. In many countries women are not permitted to own land in their own right, or to control land-use rights without the permission of a male relative. In others where, by custom or practice, they do control land or land-use, land reform is undermining their position because it introduces formal entitlements which almost invariably go to men. Land reform, an important part of many development schemes, benefits women least. Worldwide, women are losing land rights.

In many countries, women cannot inherit either property or wealth, or cannot do so on equal terms with men. In the Islamic code, a daughter's inheritance is limited to one-half of the son's share. In other countries, women are not entitled to an equal share of resources accumulated during marriage.

Women are also denied one of the most basic rights, to choose their domicile. In many countries, it is still a man's prerogative to choose where the family will live. This is usually the right of husband or father, but in some countries it may even pass to a son or a brother.

Even in countries where women are free to own productive assets, they have little and control less. In mining, manufacturing and transport, women are very nearly invisible in the upper reaches of authority. Even in the service industries, normally a more welcoming environment for women, the most important areas, like financial dealings and transactions in landed property, are almost always entirely male preserves.

LAND RIGHTS

Countries where women (or some women, living under customary or religious laws) do not have the same rights as men to own and administer their own land, or to control and administer communal, tribal or joint landed property, where known, 1980s

● women do not have same rights as men   ● unknown, unclear and others

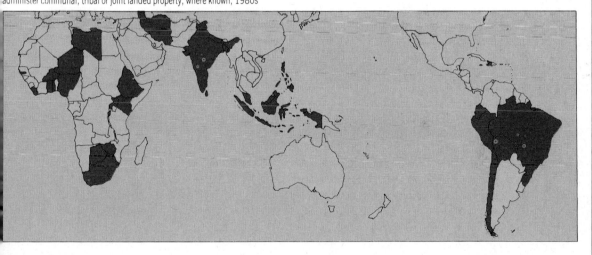

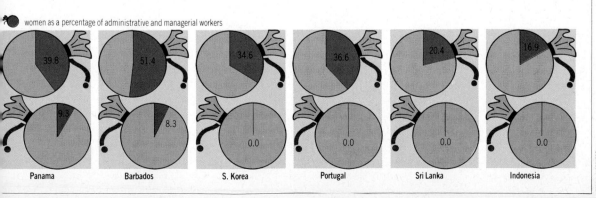

women as a percentage of administrative and managerial workers

Panama	Barbados	S. Korea	Portugal	Sri Lanka	Indonesia
39.8	51.4	34.6	36.6	20.4	16.9
9.3	8.3	0.0	0.0	0.0	0.0

BOTTOM OF THE CLASS

Countries in which girls form 35 per cent or less of all pupils in secondary schools, 1980s, where known, *percentages*

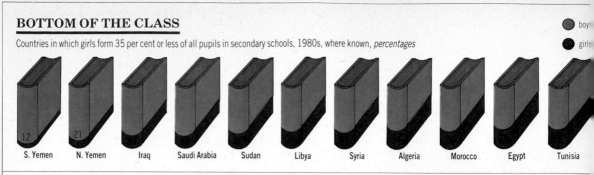

| S. Yemen | N. Yemen | Iraq | Saudi Arabia | Sudan | Libya | Syria | Algeria | Morocco | Egypt | Tunisia |

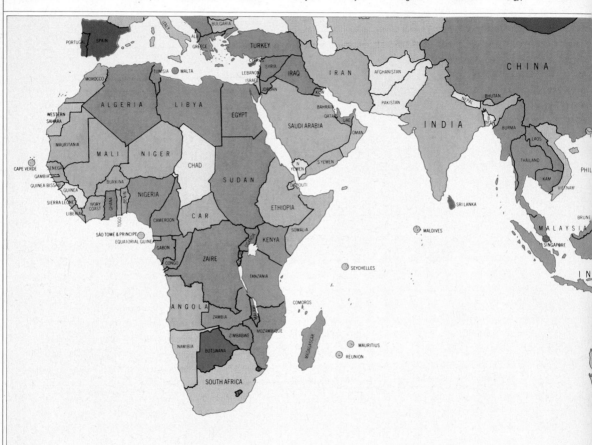

THE BIG LEAP

Relative increase in girls' enrolment over boys' enrolment, primary and secondary schools, 1960–80, 25 countries, *percentages*

740 Nepal

644 Saudi Arabia

550 Papua New Guinea

384 Chad

Education is one of the greatest forces for change for women. A woman who can read, write and add numbers has a better chance in life.

In the past twenty-five years, tremendous strides have been made in primary school enrolment; in many countries formal education is no longer seen as wasted on girls.

But the female–male gap still exists at secondary level: in 76 poor countries, less than half of eligible girls are enrolled in secondary school. Where school slots are scarce, boys must compete – but girls are not even expected to try.

Where girls do go to school, they drop out more than boys do. Especially in poor, rural settings, girls are needed at home for chores, or parents do not want their adolescent daughters to mingle with boys. The educational investment is thought to be better spent on sons.

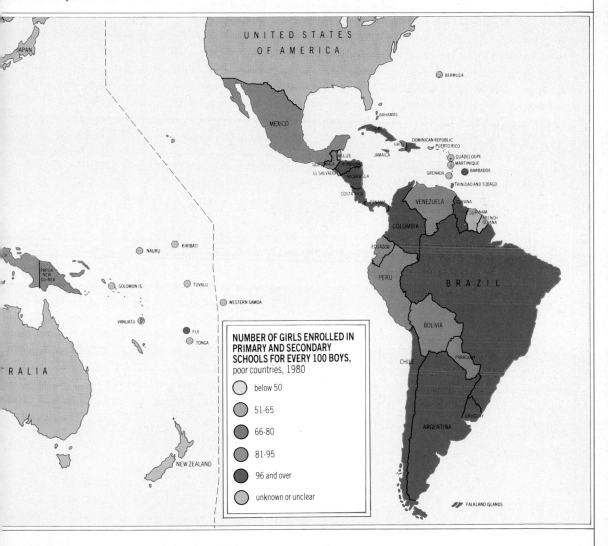

NUMBER OF GIRLS ENROLLED IN PRIMARY AND SECONDARY SCHOOLS FOR EVERY 100 BOYS,
poor countries, 1980

- below 50
- 51-65
- 66-80
- 81-95
- 96 and over
- unknown or unclear

120 N. Yemen	80 Sudan	34 India	10 South Africa (including blacks)
100 Zaire	69 Afghanistan	29 Indonesia	9 Egypt
98 Jordan	62 Bangladesh	26 Malaysia	8 S. Korea
93 Ethiopia	40 Burkina	24 Peru	4 Brazil
89 Kenya	40 Iran	21 Angola	4 Nicaragua 2 Haiti

Sources in Notes

BY DEGREES

Year of women's admission to some famous universities

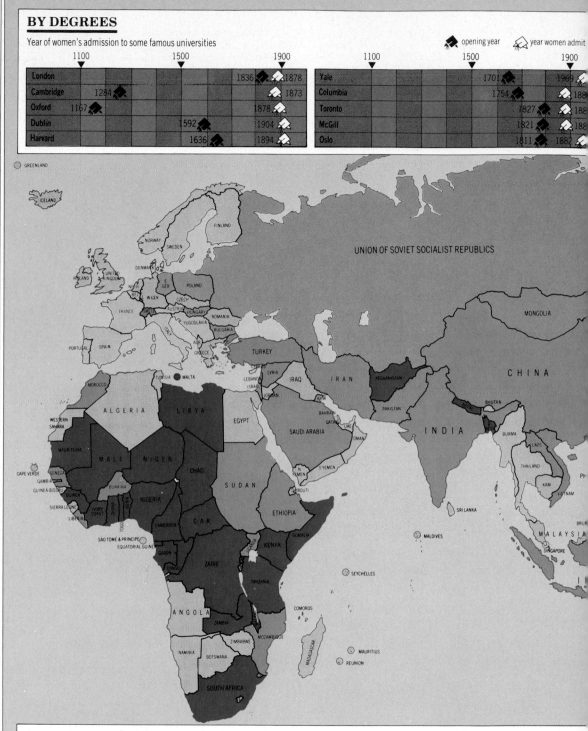

◆ opening year   ◇ year women admitted

	1100	1500	1900		1100	1500	1900
London			1836 ◆ ◇ 1878	Yale	1701 ◆		◇ 1969
Cambridge	1284 ◆		◇ 1873	Columbia		1754 ◆	◇ 188
Oxford	1167 ◆		1878 ◇	Toronto		1827 ◆	◇ 188
Dublin		1592 ◆	1904 ◇	McGill		1821 ◆	◇ 188
Harvard		1636 ◆	1894 ◇	Oslo		1811 ◆	◇ 1882

GENDER OF STUDIES

Degrees conferred on women, by field of study, USA, 1980, *percentages*

BA degree *italic*   PhD **bold**

Professional degrees conferred on women, USA, 1980, *percentages*

	BA	PhD		BA	PhD		BA	PhD		
engineering	*9*	**4**	geography	*32*	**14**	fine & applied arts	*63*	**37**	dentistry	13
physical sciences	*24*	**13**	business/management	*37*	**15**	education	*74*	**44**	theology	1
philosophy	*27*	**24**	mathematics	*42*	**14**	social work	*81*	**50**	medicine	23
computer science	*30*	**11**	social sciences	*44*	**27**	library science	*95*	**56**	law	30

For women to perform effectively in a world of professionals, they need access to higher education. While girls have made great progress in school enrolment, almost nowhere do women match men on the university campus. This is true despite dramatic enrolment increases in some countries.

Often, women cannot afford to go to university, do not believe in their own abilities, and are not encouraged to succeed academically. Where women do attend, they are often encouraged into female disciplinary ghettos such as social work, education and library science. This is now beginning to change, however, as more and more women turn to the sciences and enter the professions.

The oldest and most famous universities long excluded women. It is only recently, since the wave of women's liberation at the turn of the century, that women have appeared on campus at all.

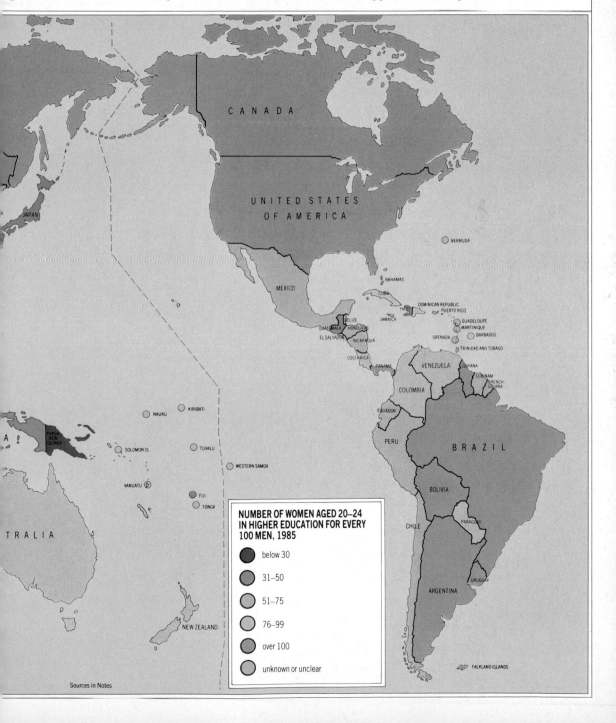

NUMBER OF WOMEN AGED 20–24 IN HIGHER EDUCATION FOR EVERY 100 MEN, 1985

- below 30
- 31–50
- 51–75
- 76–99
- over 100
- unknown or unclear

Sources in Notes

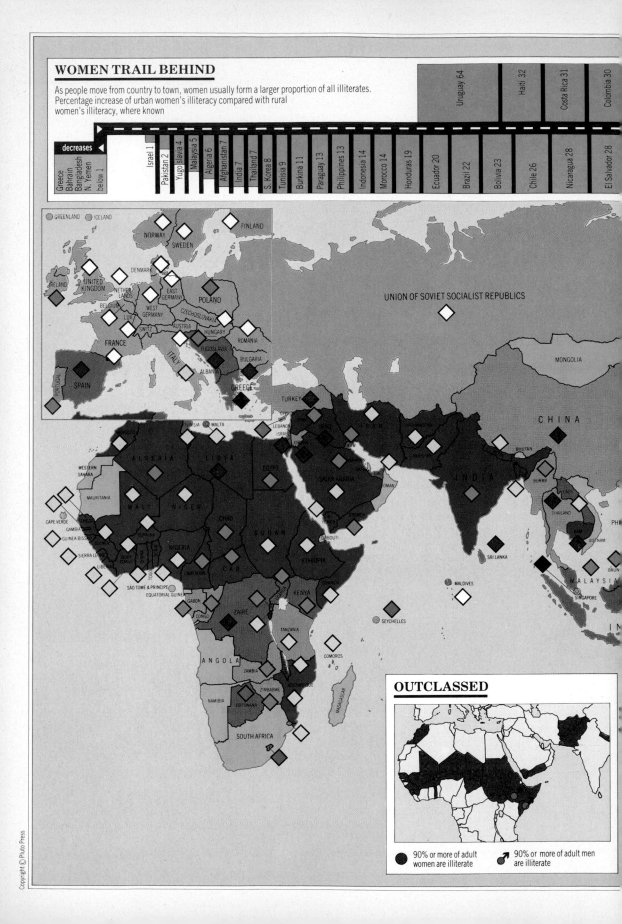

WOMEN TRAIL BEHIND

As people move from country to town, women usually form a larger proportion of all illiterates. Percentage increase of urban women's illiteracy compared with rural women's illiteracy, where known

decreases ◀

| Greece Bahrain Bangladesh N. Yemen below 1 | Israel 1 | Pakistan 2 | Yugo Slavia 4 | Malaysia 5 | Algeria 6 | Afghanistan 7 | India 7 | Thailand 7 | S. Korea 8 | Tunisia 9 | Burkina 11 | Paraguay 13 | Philippines 13 | Indonesia 14 | Morocco 14 | Honduras 19 | Ecuador 20 | Brazil 22 | Bolivia 23 | Chile 26 | Nicaragua 28 | El Salvador 28 |

| Uruguay 64 | Haiti 32 | Costa Rica 31 | Colombia 30 |

GREENLAND   ICELAND

NORWAY   FINLAND
SWEDEN
DENMARK
IRELAND
UNITED KINGDOM   NETHER-LANDS   EAST GERMANY   POLAND
BELGIUM   WEST GERMANY   CZECHOSLOVAKIA
LUX.   AUSTRIA   HUNGARY
SWITZ.
FRANCE   ROMANIA
ITALY   YUGOSLAVIA   BULGARIA
ALBANIA
PORTUGAL   SPAIN   GREECE

UNION OF SOVIET SOCIALIST REPUBLICS

TURKEY
CYPRUS
LEBANON   IRAQ   IRAN
ISRAEL   JORDAN
TUNISIA   MALTA   KUWAIT   AFGHANISTAN
MOROCCO   QATAR   PAKISTAN   BHUTAN
ALGERIA   LIBYA   EGYPT   SAUDI ARABIA   U.A.E.   INDIA   BURMA
OMAN   LAOS
WESTERN SAHARA   THAILAND
MAURITANIA   NIGER   CHAD   SUDAN   YEMEN
MALI   DJIBOUTI
CAPE VERDE   SENEGAL   ETHIOPIA   VIETNAM
GAMBIA   BURKINA   NIGERIA   SRI LANKA
GUINEA-BISSAU   BENIN   MALDIVES   MALAYSIA
SIERRA LEONE   IVORY COAST   GHANA   CAR   SOMALIA   SINGAPORE
LIBERIA   TOGO   CAMEROON   KENYA
SÃO TOMÉ & PRINCIPE   GABON   CONGO
EQUATORIAL GUINEA   ZAIRE   SEYCHELLES
TANZANIA
COMOROS
ANGOLA   ZAMBIA
MOZAMBIQUE
NAMIBIA   ZIMBABWE   MADAGASCAR
BOTSWANA

SOUTH AFRICA

MONGOLIA   CHINA

BRUN

OUTCLASSED

● 90% or more of adult women are illiterate

↗ 90% or more of adult men are illiterate

Adults who can neither read nor write also cannot participate fully in modern life. More adult women than men fall into this category: two-thirds of the world's illiterates are women; in seventeen countries over 90 per cent of women are illiterate.

This is largely the legacy of women's relative confinement to domestic and private life, and the widespread prejudice against educating girls.

Almost everywhere the gap in literacy between women and men is widening. This is especially true in cities, where men have more opportunities – often at work – to learn to read and write. So, while literacy for both women and men is higher in cities than in rural areas, urbanization more often than not leaves women at a relative disadvantage. Women's illiteracy is also more hidden than men's, and official figures are known to underestimate the problem.

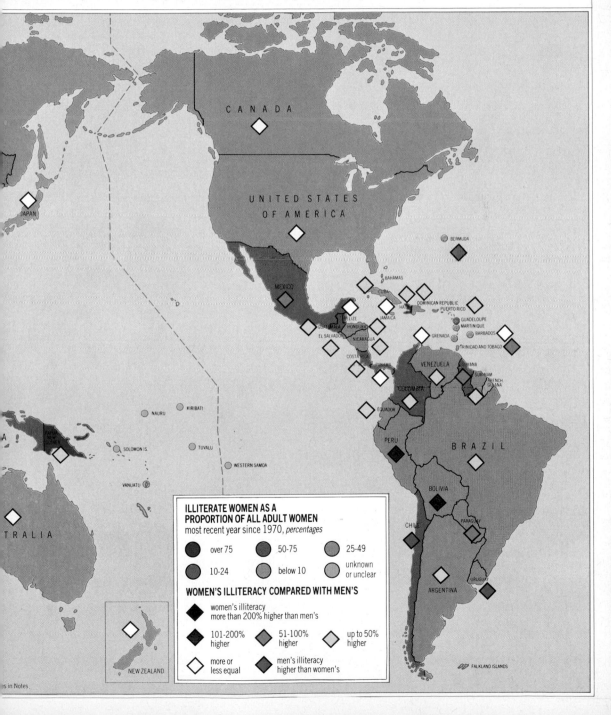

ILLITERATE WOMEN AS A PROPORTION OF ALL ADULT WOMEN
most recent year since 1970, *percentages*

- over 75
- 50-75
- 25-49
- 10-24
- below 10
- unknown or unclear

WOMEN'S ILLITERACY COMPARED WITH MEN'S

- women's illiteracy more than 200% higher than men's
- 101-200% higher
- 51-100% higher
- up to 50% higher
- more or less equal
- men's illiteracy higher than women's

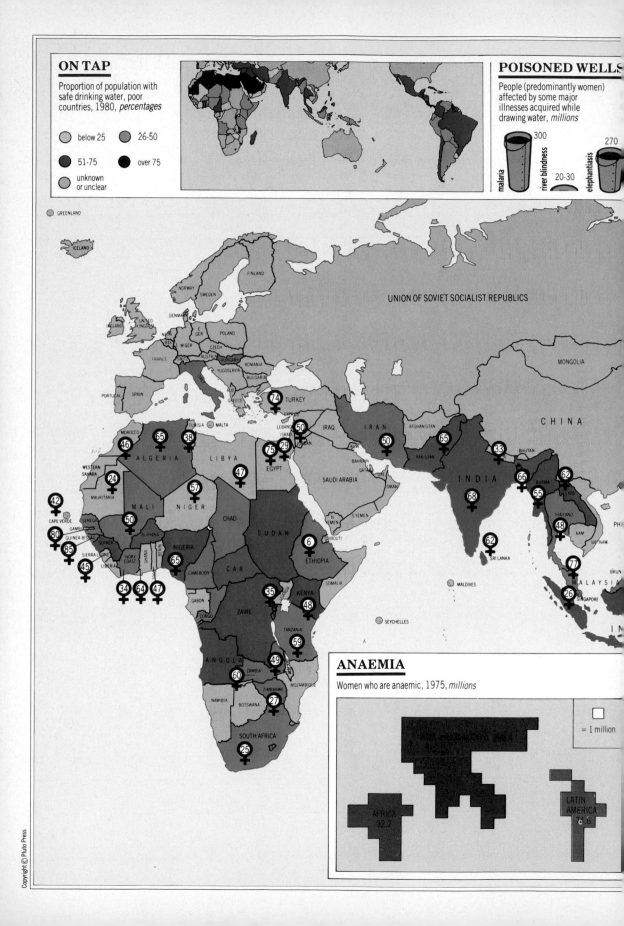

ON TAP

Proportion of population with
safe drinking water, poor
countries, 1980, *percentages*

- below 25
- 26-50
- 51-75
- over 75
- unknown
or unclear

POISONED WELLS

People (predominantly women)
affected by some major
illnesses acquired while
drawing water, *millions*

malaria 300

river blindness 20-30

elephantiasis 270

ANAEMIA

Women who are anaemic, 1975, *millions*

☐ = 1 million

ASIA excluding China 206.4

AFRICA 92.2

LATIN AMERICA 74.6

UNION OF SOVIET SOCIALIST REPUBLICS

CHINA

MONGOLIA

INDIA

The world's women are chronically fatigued, and many are anaemic from malnourishment. This means that when women are exposed to disease they are especially susceptible.

It is women who collect, cook with, and wash family and home using local water. If the water source is far away, unclean, or in short supply, it is primarily women who suffer from the resulting fatigue and disease. And it is women who are held responsible for the poor health of their families when polluted water and inadequate sanitation make the practice of good hygiene either difficult or well-nigh impossible.

Women sow, reap, harvest and cook the world's food, but serve themselves last and least. When food is scarce, women suffer most and future generations are handicapped from birth by malnourished pregnant and nursing mothers.

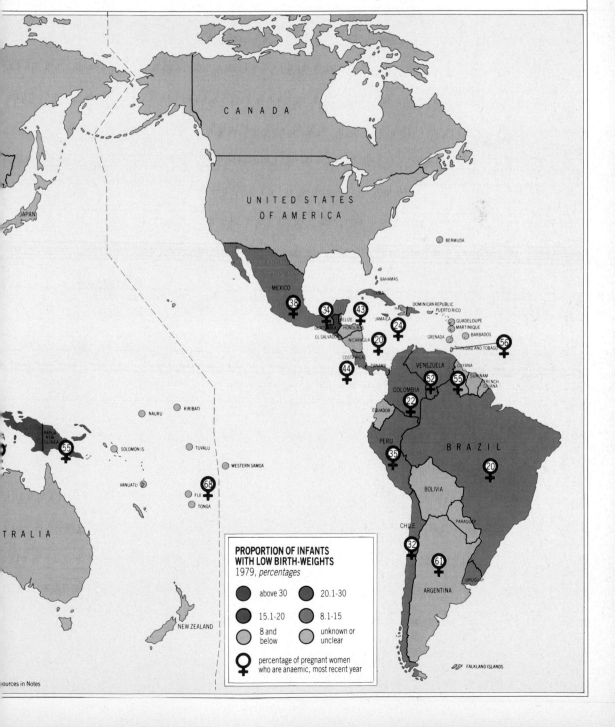

PROPORTION OF INFANTS WITH LOW BIRTH-WEIGHTS
1979, percentages

- above 30
- 20.1-30
- 15.1-20
- 8.1-15
- 8 and below
- unknown or unclear

♀ percentage of pregnant women who are anaemic, most recent year

Sources in Notes

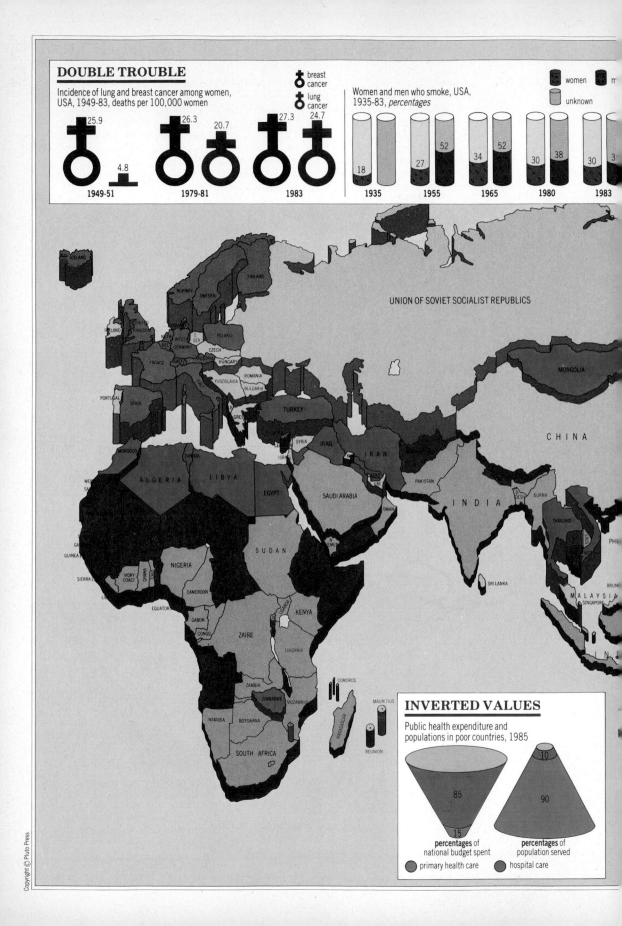

DOUBLE TROUBLE

Incidence of lung and breast cancer among women, USA, 1949-83, deaths per 100,000 women

♀ breast cancer
♀ lung cancer

25.9		26.3	20.7	27.3	24.7
1949-51		**1979-81**		**1983**	

Women and men who smoke, USA, 1935-83, *percentages*

women   m
unknown

1935	1955	1965	1980	1983
18	27	52	34	52	30	38	30	3

UNION OF SOVIET SOCIALIST REPUBLICS

ICELAND
FINLAND
NORWAY
SWEDEN
IRELAND
UNITED KINGDOM
NETH
BEL
W.GER
E.GER
POLAND
CZECH
FRANCE
SWITZ
AUSTRIA
HUNGARY
ITALY
YUGOSLAVIA
ROMANIA
BULGARIA
PORTUGAL
SPAIN
GREECE
TURKEY
MONGOLIA
MOROCCO
TUNISIA
SYRIA
IRAQ
ISRAEL
IRAN
CHINA
ALGERIA
LIBYA
EGYPT
SAUDI ARABIA
QATAR
UAE
PAKISTAN
WEST SAH
OMAN
INDIA
B'DESH
BURMA
GA
GUINEA-B
SUDAN
YEMEN
SIERRA L
IVORY COAST
GHANA
TOGO
NIGERIA
CAMEROON
THAILAND
PHI
SRI LANKA
VIETNAM
EQUATOR
GABON
CONGO
UGANDA
KENYA
BRUN
MALAYSIA
SINGAPORE
ZAIRE
TANZANIA
IND
COMOROS
ZAMBIA
MAURITIUS
ZIMBABWE
MOZAMBIQUE
MADAGASCAR
NAMIBIA
BOTSWANA
REUNION
SOUTH AFRICA

INVERTED VALUES

Public health expenditure and populations in poor countries, 1985

85
15
10
90

percentages of national budget spent

percentages of population served

● primary health care   ● hospital care

Women are biologically stronger than men. But where girls' and women's health is neglected, that edge is lost. In poor countries and in rural settings, constant childbearing, lack of village-level health care, and the neglect of infant girls in favour of boys, all make living more hazardous for women.

Working harder and longer, eating less and worse, earning less and having little control over resources – all while giving birth and nursing – make women more vulnerable to disease. This is particularly true in poor countries, where death from infectious and parasitic disease is prevalent.

In the rich world, where women live long enough to develop degenerative and environmental diseases, they are increasingly taking the same chances as men – smoking, drinking and taking drugs – and are increasingly in danger from cancer, heart disease and strokes.

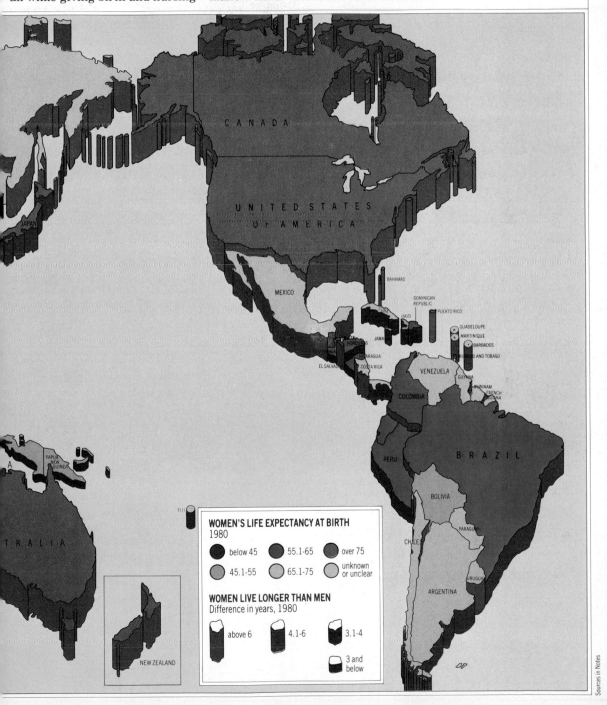

WOMEN'S LIFE EXPECTANCY AT BIRTH
1980

- below 45
- 55.1-65
- over 75
- 45.1-55
- 65.1-75
- unknown or unclear

WOMEN LIVE LONGER THAN MEN
Difference in years, 1980

- above 6
- 4.1-6
- 3.1-4
- 3 and below

It is war, famine, drought, and oppression that turn people into international refugees. There are now over 15 million refugees in the world; the large majority are women and their dependent children.

Refugees often escape from one state of misery only to enter another of equal, if not greater misery. Countries of asylum are often as poor as the countries they flee. Women often flee from one country where their status is low, to another where it is no better; as refugees, they sink even lower. Refugee women are among the poorest of the world's poor, and they have little control over their fate: women generally have no say in the administration of refugee camps, or in the development of national and international refugee policies.

With no protection of family or state, women refugees are under constant threats – of which rape is the most generally pervasive.

PEOPLE IN EXILE

Refugees of the 1980s

AFGHANISTAN TO:

Turkey 1,000   Iran 1,5 million

Pakistan 2,9 million

India 5-50,000   Egypt 5-50,000

ETHIOPIA TO:

Italy 5,000   N. Yemen 5,000   Egypt 2,000   Djibouti 23,000   Somalia 700,000

Sudan 500,000

Kenya below 3,000   Uganda above 50,000

VIETNAM TO:

Canada 123,000   Japan 2,100

USA, Thailand, Australia 50,000-250,000 each

Hong Kong, Indonesia, New Zealand 5-50,000 each

EL SALVADOR TO:

Mexico 170,000

USA below 5,000   Guatemala 70,000   Honduras 22,000

Belize 7,000   Nicaragua 18,500   Costa Rica 8,000   Panama 1,500

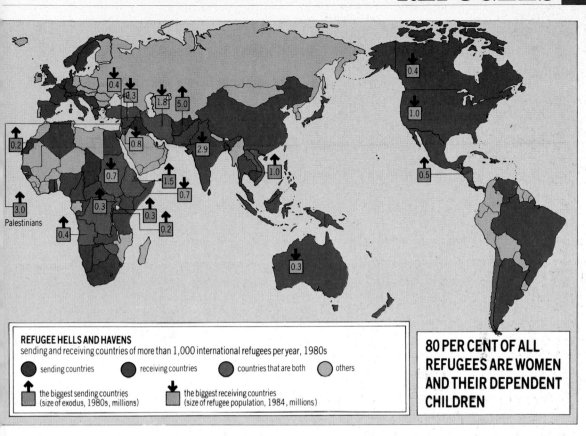

REFUGEE HELLS AND HAVENS
sending and receiving countries of more than 1,000 international refugees per year, 1980s

● sending countries   ● receiving countries   ● countries that are both   ○ others

↑ the biggest sending countries
(size of exodus, 1980s, millions)

↓ the biggest receiving countries
(size of refugee population, 1984, millions)

80 PER CENT OF ALL REFUGEES ARE WOMEN AND THEIR DEPENDENT CHILDREN

THE PALESTINIAN EXILES

The number of Palestinian refugees in the 1980s

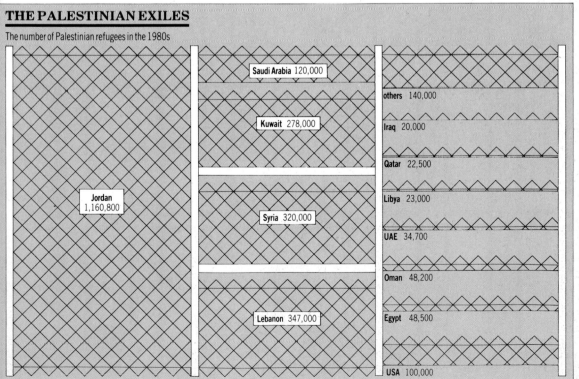

Jordan 1,160,800

Saudi Arabia 120,000
Kuwait 278,000
Syria 320,000
Lebanon 347,000

others 140,000
Iraq 20,000
Qatar 22,500
Libya 23,000
UAE 34,700
Oman 48,200
Egypt 48,500
USA 100,000

Sources in Notes

ALL IN THE FAMILY

Single-parent families headed by women as a proportion of all families, USA, 1984, *percentages*

all · whites · blacks · Hispanics

POOR FAMILIES

Proportion of families categorized as poor by the government, USA, 1981, *percentages*

	all	white	black	Hispanic
single-parent families headed by women	35	27	53	53
single-parent families headed by men	10	9	19	19
husband-wife families	7	6	15	15

LIVING LONGER

Proportions of women and men over aged 60, selected examples, 1985, *percentages*

women · men

	women	men
Australia	13	16
Austria	15	24
El Salvador	5	6
Finland	13	21
France	15	20
India	6	6
Indonesia	5	6
Japan	12	16
Kenya	3	3
Poland	11	16
Singapore	7	8
Sweden	21	25
Switzerland	21	27
Syria	4	5
UK	17	23
USA	14	18

Women everywhere control fewer resources and reap a lesser share of the world's wealth than men; it follows from this that when women have to support families and themselves on their own, they end up poorer than men.

In the USA, 78 per cent of all people living in poverty are women or children under 18 years old. Statistics from all over the world tell the same story: no matter how poverty is measured, the poor popula-tion is largely and increasingly comprised of women and their dependent children. This is what is known as the feminization of poverty.

Worldwide, one-third of all households are now headed by women. Women outlive men and com-monly spend some of their older years alone.

The poverty that is disproportionately borne by women, is especially borne by those with children and by older women.

FAMILIES OF WOMEN

Number of households headed by women as a proportion of all households, most recent year since mid-1970s, *percentages*

below 10   10-20   21-30   31 and above

Guinea	Iran	Jordan	Netherlands	Niger	Burkina	Italy
Argentina	Brazil	Canada	Costa Rica	Cuba	Ecuador	Finland
France	Indonesia	South Korea	Liberia	Madagascar	Malaysia	Mali
Mexico	Morocco	Poland	Sri Lanka	Syria	Taiwan	Thailand
USA	UK	Tunisia	Turkey	Zambia	Belize	El Salvador
Ghana	Guyana	Malawi	Mauritania	Rwanda	Sudan	Trinidad & Tobago
Venezuela	Barbados	Botswana	Denmark	Dominica	Honduras	Jamaica
Kenya	Lesotho	Nicaragua	Panama	Paraguay	Vietnam	Zimbabwe

Sources in Notes

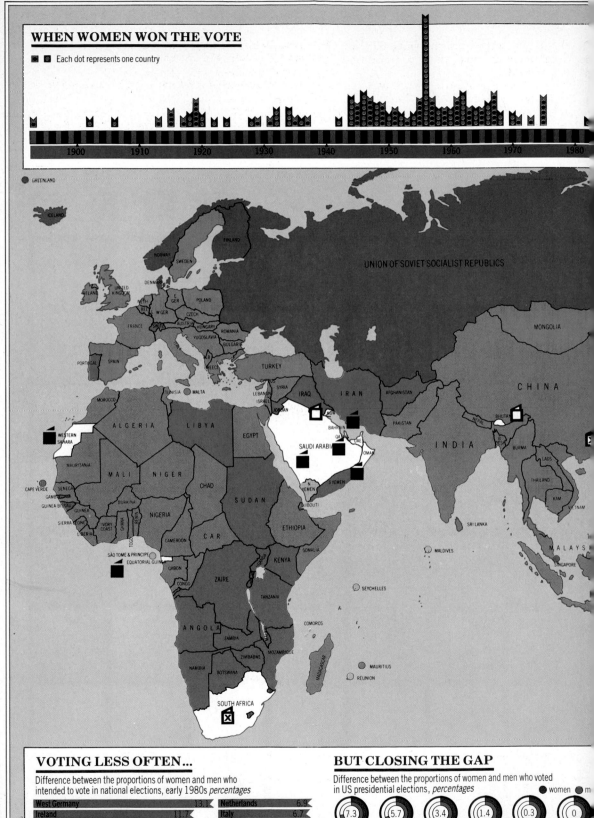

WHEN WOMEN WON THE VOTE

▓ ▣ Each dot represents one country

1900　　1910　　1920　　1930　　1940　　1950　　1960　　1970　　1980

GREENLAND

ICELAND

FINLAND

NORWAY

SWEDEN

DENMARK

IRELAND

UNITED KINGDOM

NTH
BEL

E
GER

POLAND

W GER

CZECH

FRANCE

SWITZ

AUSTRIA

HUNGARY

ROMANIA

YUGOSLAVIA

BULGARIA

PORTUGAL

SPAIN

ITALY

GREECE

TURKEY

UNION OF SOVIET SOCIALIST REPUBLICS

MONGOLIA

CHINA

CYPRUS

LEBANON

SYRIA

ISRAEL

JORDAN

IRAQ

KUW

IRAN

AFGHANISTAN

PAKISTAN

NEPAL

BHUTAN

BANGLADESH

BURMA

LAOS

TUNISIA

MALTA

MOROCCO

ALGERIA

LIBYA

EGYPT

SAUDI ARABIA

BAHRAIN

QATAR

UAE

OMAN

N YEMEN

S YEMEN

INDIA

WESTERN SAHARA

MAURITANIA

MALI

NIGER

CHAD

SUDAN

CAPE VERDE

SENEGAL

GAMBIA

GUINEA BISSAU

GUINEA

BURKINA

BENIN

NIGERIA

DJIBOUTI

ETHIOPIA

SRI LANKA

THAILAND

KAM

VIETNAM

MALAYS

SIERRA LEONE

IVORY COAST

LIBERIA

GHANA

TOGO

CAMEROON

CAR

SOMALIA

SÃO TOME & PRINCIPE

EQUATORIAL GUINEA

GABON

CONGO

ZAIRE

KENYA

RWANDA

TANZANIA

MALDIVES

SINGAPORE

SEYCHELLES

ANGOLA

ZAMBIA

ZIMBABWE

MOZAMBIQUE

COMOROS

NAMIBIA

BOTSWANA

MADAGASCAR

MAURITIUS

RÉUNION

SOUTH AFRICA

VOTING LESS OFTEN...

Difference between the proportions of women and men who intended to vote in national elections, early 1980s *percentages*

West Germany	13.1	Netherlands	6.9
Ireland	11.7	Italy	6.7
Denmark	8.0	UK	2.7
Greece	7.2	France	2.6

BUT CLOSING THE GAP

Difference between the proportions of women and men who voted in US presidential elections, *percentages*

● women ● m

7.3	5.7	3.4	1.4	0.3	0
1964	1968	1972	1976	1980	19

The right to vote is an important measure of full citizenship, and an important means for women to gain other rights.

Voting rights for women were often strongly resisted almost everywhere, and men gained the vote before women; in a few countries this is still so. In some countries, white women or women with property or education had the vote before others. In many, women won the vote as part of a larger social reordering, such as the transfer from colonial to national rule. For many women, then, voting is a recent privilege.

Worldwide, women tend to vote less than men, but the gap is narrowing.

Since women everywhere are a slight majority of the population, if women voted in equal proportion to men they would actually represent an electoral majority.

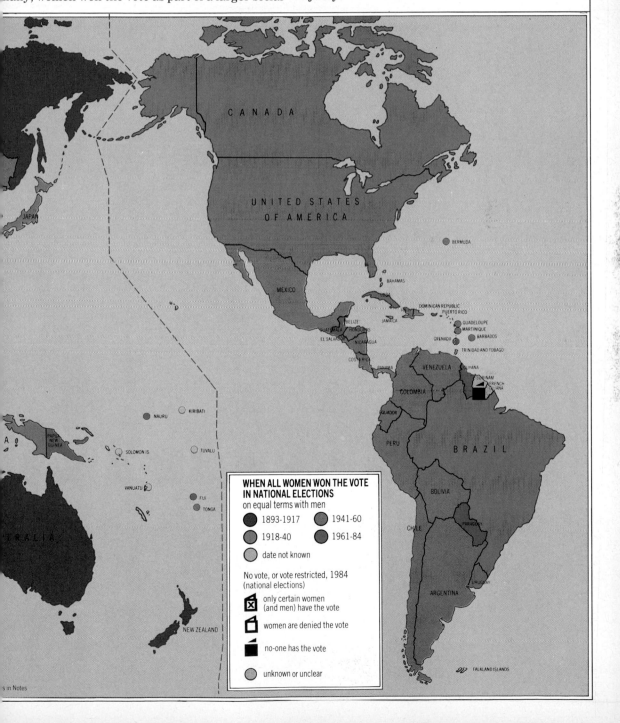

WHEN ALL WOMEN WON THE VOTE IN NATIONAL ELECTIONS
on equal terms with men

- 1893-1917
- 1918-40
- 1941-60
- 1961-84
- date not known

No vote, or vote restricted, 1984 (national elections)

- ⊠ only certain women (and men) have the vote
- ⬜ women are denied the vote
- ◼ no-one has the vote
- unknown or unclear

s in Notes

Most governments are governments of men. Nowhere do women hold more than a minority of seats in national legislatures. In many of the countries where they appear to have a greater voice, the legislatures they serve are in fact powerless or symbolic. There are only a handful of countries in which women have significant representation in a significant legislature. In Scandinavia, women have the best – and the earliest – record of representation in government.

That women have the right to participate in government does not mean they exercise much power in most countries. The gender gap in government is greatest at the top of the hierarchy. The powerful and prestigious government posts are typically held by men across the entire spectrum of political systems. Women in cabinet-level positions remain exceptions to the rule everywhere.

THE GATES OPEN SLOWLY

Date of women's first entry into high-level political positions compared with date of first suffrage, selected examples

date of first suffrage · first woman to cabinet post

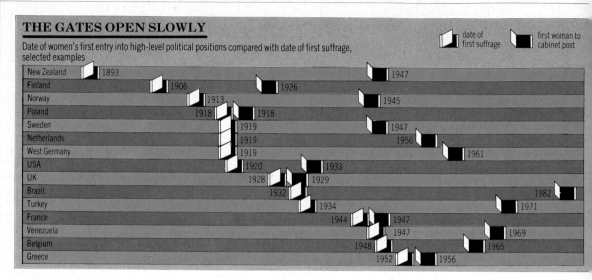

EARLY MOMENTUM

Early growth of women's representation in national legislatures, Scandinavia *percentages*

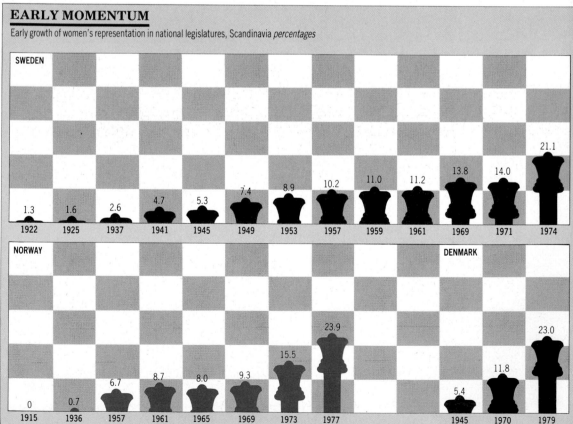

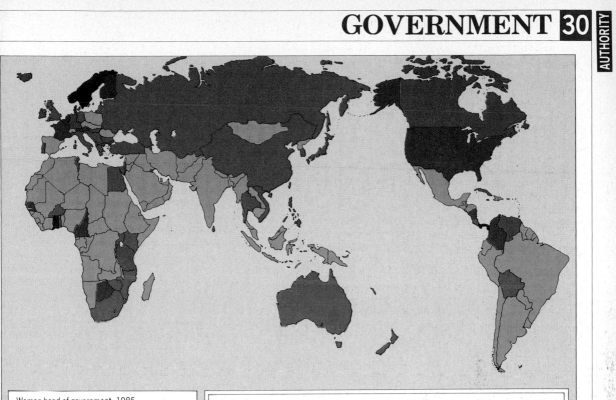

Woman head of government, 1985

 Iceland, United Kingdom,
Yugoslavia, Dominica

WOMEN IN THE EXECUTIVE (CABINET LEVEL) BRANCH OF GOVERNMENT, 1984 *percentages*

● above 20   ▨ 11-20   ◗ 6-10   ◖ 5 and below   ○ unknown
or unclear

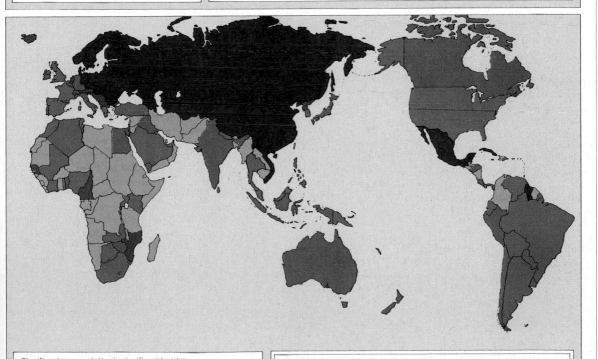

Significant representation in significant legislature

 Denmark, Norway, Sweden, Finland

WOMEN IN THE LEGISLATIVE BRANCH OF GOVERNMENT, 1984 *percentages*

● above 20   ● 11-20   ● 6-10   ● 5 and below   ○ unknown
or unclear

Sources in Notes

THE CRIMINAL ELEMENTS

Women and men compared, UK, USA and Sweden, early 1980s, *percentages*

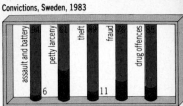

● women ● men

Prison sentences, UK, 1982

burglary 99	robbery 98	theft, fraud and forgery 95	violence against the person 98
1	2	5	2

Arrests, USA, 1983

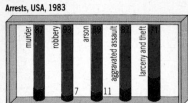

murder 87	robbery 93	arson 89	aggravated assault 87	larceny and theft 71
		7	11	

Convictions, Sweden, 1983

assault and battery 94	petty larceny 61	theft 89	fraud 78	drug offences 85
	6		11	

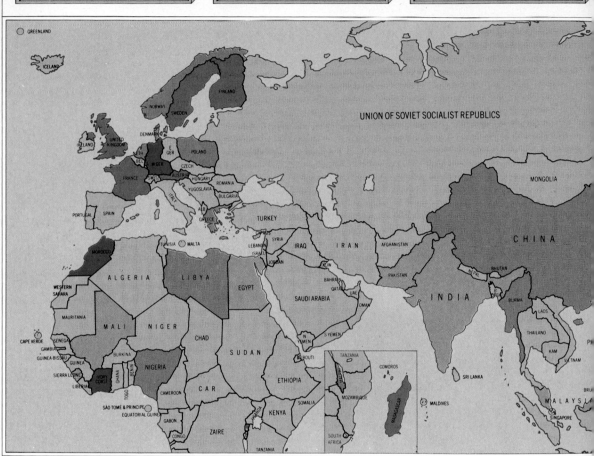

GREENLAND

ICELAND

NORWAY

FINLAND

SWEDEN

UNION OF SOVIET SOCIALIST REPUBLICS

IRELAND

UNITED KINGDOM

DENMARK

NETH BEL

W GER

E GER

POLAND

FRANCE

SWITZ

AUSTRIA

CZECH

HUNGARY

ROMANIA

YUGOSLAVIA

BULGARIA

ALB

GREECE

MONGOLIA

PORTUGAL

SPAIN

ITALY

TUNISIA

MALTA

TURKEY

CYPRUS

SYRIA

LEBANON

ISRAEL

JORDAN

IRAQ

IRAN

AFGHANISTAN

CHINA

MOROCCO

ALGERIA

LIBYA

EGYPT

SAUDI ARABIA

KUW

BAHRAIN

QATAR

UAE

OMAN

PAKISTAN

NEPAL

BHUTAN

B DESH

INDIA

BURMA

LAOS

WESTERN SAHARA

MAURITANIA

MALI

NIGER

CHAD

SUDAN

N YEMEN

S YEMEN

THAILAND

KAM

VIETNAM

CAPE VERDE

SENEGAL

GAMBIA

GUINEA-BISSAU

GUINEA

SIERRA LEONE

LIBERIA

IVORY COAST

GHANA

TOGO

BENIN

NIGERIA

CAR

CAMEROON

ETHIOPIA

DJIBOUTI

SOMALIA

TANZANIA

COMOROS

SRI LANKA

MALDIVES

MALAYSIA

SINGAPORE

BRU

SÃO TOMÉ & PRINCIPE

EQUATORIAL GUINEA

GABON

CONGO

ZAIRE

RWANDA

BURUNDI

KENYA

TANZANIA

MOZAMBIQUE

MADAGASCAR

SOUTH AFRICA

BARRED WOMEN

Women as a proportion of all lawyers, where data is known, early 1980s, *percentages*

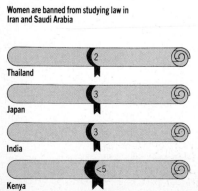

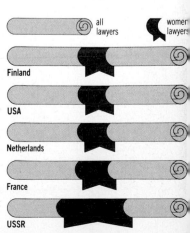

all lawyers

women lawyers

Women are banned from studying law in Iran and Saudi Arabia

Thailand 2

Japan 3

India 3

Kenya <5

Syria <5

Spain 6

Italy

Portugal

Bulgaria

Finland

USA

Netherlands

France

USSR

There are wide differences in how 'crimes' and 'criminals' are officially defined and reported. But, regardless of definition, most crimes are committed by men, and everywhere, women constitute a very small proportion of all criminals.

In most countries, women's crime rates are now increasing rapidly and at a much faster rate than men's. But women's share of total crimes remains minor.

The gap between women and men is greatest in violent crimes. Typically, more than 90 per cent of incidents involving violence are committed by men. Theft and larceny are the crimes most commonly attributed to women.

Women have very little representation in the administration of law. They are banned from studying law in two countries, but in general they are a small and growing proportion of all lawyers.

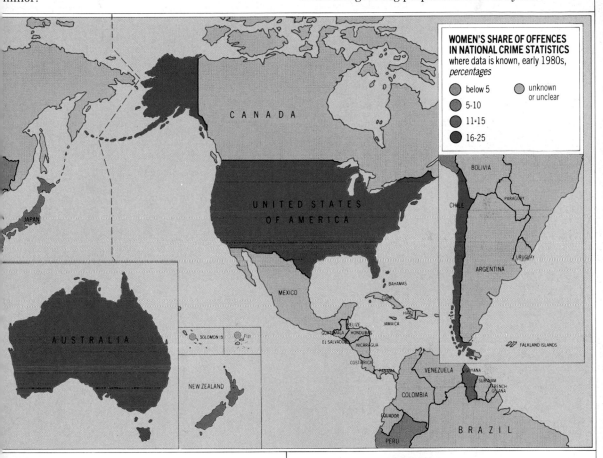

WOMEN'S SHARE OF OFFENCES IN NATIONAL CRIME STATISTICS
where data is known, early 1980s, *percentages*

- below 5
- 5-10
- 11·15
- 16-25
- unknown or unclear

ARRESTING WOMEN

Percentage increase in the number of arrests of women and men, 1969-78, USA, *percentages*

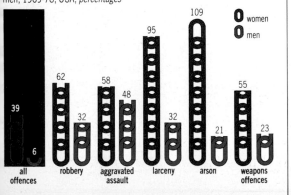

- women
- men

	all offences	robbery	aggravated assault	larceny	arson	weapons offences
women	39	62	58	95	109	55
men	6	32	48	32	21	23

WOMEN IN TROUBLE

UK
crimes of women prisoners, 1982, *percentages*
- 56, 27, 17
- crimes against property
- crimes against persons
- other

Sweden
crimes of convicted women, 1983, *percentages*
- 36, 42, 19, 3
- crimes against property
- motoring offences
- crimes against persons
- other

India
crimes of women arrested, 1975, *percentages*
- 51, 19, 8
- theft
- riot
- crimes against persons
- other

Sources in Notes

WOMEN FIGHTERS

Countries where women have been combatants in revolutionary armies and civil wars, where known, 1975-85

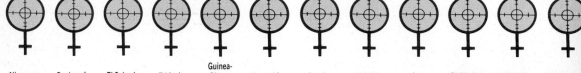

| Nicaragua | Guatemala | El Salvador | Ethiopia | Guinea-Bissau | Mozambique | Angola | Namibia | Iran | Philippines | Vietnam | Zimbabwe |

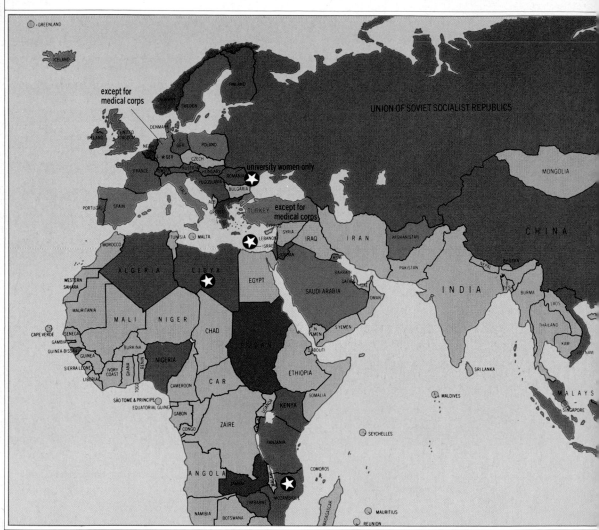

except for medical corps

university women only

except for medical corps

UNION OF SOVIET SOCIALIST REPUBLICS

WOMEN IN NATO

Percentage of women in armed forces of NATO countries, 1983

● men ● women * medical corps officers only

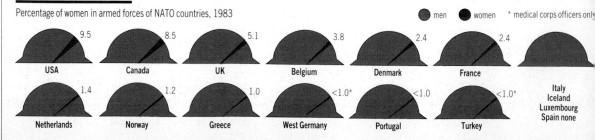

USA	Canada	UK	Belgium	Denmark	France	
9.5	8.5	5.1	3.8	2.4	2.4	
Netherlands	Norway	Greece	West Germany	Portugal	Turkey	Italy Iceland Luxembourg Spain none
1.4	1.2	1.0	<1.0*	<1.0	<1.0*	

Serving one's country as part of the military is widely held to be an honour and an act of patriotism. Military service also brings economic and social rewards, especially in countries where the armed forces are politically powerful or where they form the government.

Most governments do not want women in their armed forces. But many now feel that they are running short on acceptable male recruits. So an uneasy compromise adopted in many countries is to permit women into the services, but to deny them certain roles. Combat, in particular, is considered unnatural for women, although large numbers of them have fought in civil wars and revolutionary armies.

In wartime, even the regular armies resort to using women in service, but after the war they are expected to return home.

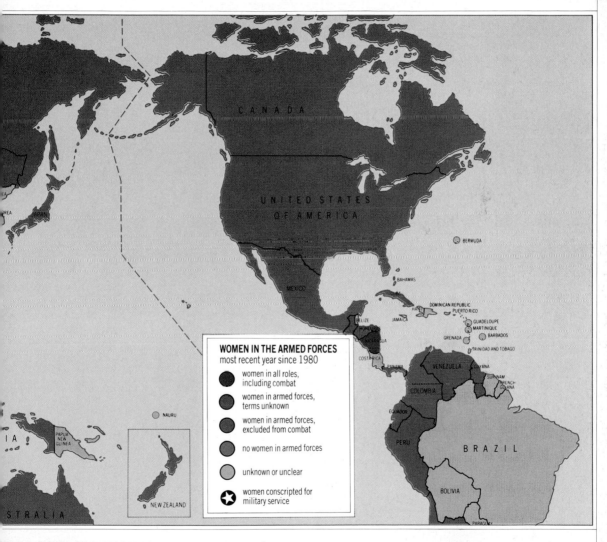

WOMEN IN THE ARMED FORCES
most recent year since 1980

- women in all roles, including combat
- women in armed forces, terms unknown
- women in armed forces, excluded from combat
- no women in armed forces
- unknown or unclear
- women conscripted for military service

WARTIME WARRIORS

Women in the armed forces of the UK, 1939-46

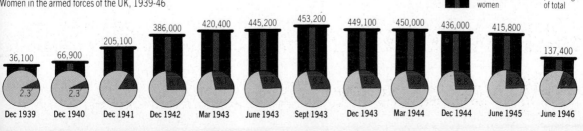

number of women · women as percentage of total

Dec 1939	Dec 1940	Dec 1941	Dec 1942	Mar 1943	June 1943	Sept 1943	Dec 1943	Mar 1944	Dec 1944	June 1945	June 1946
36,100	66,900	205,100	386,000	420,400	445,200	453,200	449,100	450,000	436,000	415,800	137,400
2.3	2.3										

Sources in Notes

WOMEN DO MOST OF THE WORK

Number of women health care workers (nurses and doctors) for every 100 men health care workers
selected examples, most recent year since 1975

⬤ 100 women health care workers

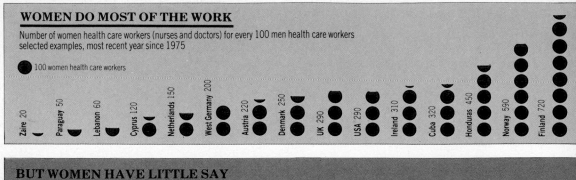

| Zaire 20 | Paraguay 50 | Lebanon 60 | Cyprus 120 | Netherlands 150 | West Germany 200 | Austria 220 | Denmark 250 | UK 290 | USA 290 | Ireland 310 | Cuba 320 | Honduras 450 | Norway 590 | Finland 720 |

BUT WOMEN HAVE LITTLE SAY

where data is known, most recent year since 1975

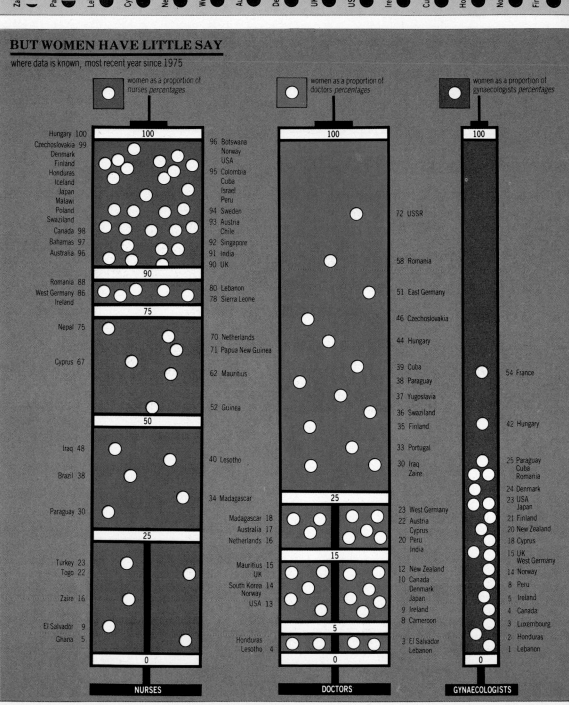

women as a proportion of nurses *percentages*

women as a proportion of doctors *percentages*

women as a proportion of gynaecologists *percentages*

NURSES

Hungary 100	
Czechoslovakia 99	96 Botswana / Norway / USA
Denmark	95 Colombia / Cuba / Israel / Peru
Finland	
Honduras	
Iceland	
Japan	
Malawi	
Poland	94 Sweden
Swaziland	93 Austria / Chile
Canada 98	92 Singapore
Bahamas 97	91 India
Australia 96	90 UK
Romania 88	80 Lebanon
West Germany 86	78 Sierra Leone
Ireland	
Nepal 75	70 Netherlands / 71 Papua New Guinea
Cyprus 67	62 Mauritius
	52 Guinea
Iraq 48	40 Lesotho
Brazil 38	
Paraguay 30	34 Madagascar
Turkey 23	
Togo 22	
Zaire 16	
El Salvador 9	
Ghana 5	

DOCTORS

	72 USSR
	58 Romania
	51 East Germany
	46 Czechoslovakia
	44 Hungary
	39 Cuba
	38 Paraguay
	37 Yugoslavia
	36 Swaziland
	35 Finland
	33 Portugal
	30 Iraq / Zaire
	23 West Germany
Madagascar 18	22 Austria / Cyprus
Australia 17	20 Peru / India
Netherlands 16	
Mauritius 15 / UK	12 New Zealand
South Korea 14 / Norway	10 Canada / Denmark / Japan
USA 13	9 Ireland
	8 Cameroon
Honduras / Lesotho 4	3 El Salvador / Lebanon

GYNAECOLOGISTS

	54 France
	42 Hungary
	25 Paraguay / Cuba / Romania
	24 Denmark
	23 USA / Japan
	21 Finland
	20 New Zealand
	18 Cyprus
	15 UK / West Germany
	14 Norway
	8 Peru
	5 Ireland
	4 Canada
	3 Luxembourg
	2 Honduras
	1 Lebanon

Women constitute by far the greater number of health care workers in most countries, but they are not represented evenly throughout the profession. They are concentrated mostly in one sector: nursing, which being 'women's work', is accorded the lowest pay, the least prestige and the least power. So while they do the greater share of health care work, women receive the smaller share of benefits.

The status, pay and power imbalance in health care is shifting slowly as more women become doctors, and as nurses press demands for better recognition of the work they do. But the gap is still large, even in that part of the profession that deals exclusively with women, gynaecology.

The picture is much the same in teaching. Most teachers in the world are women, but most women teachers occupy the bottom rung of the educational ladder.

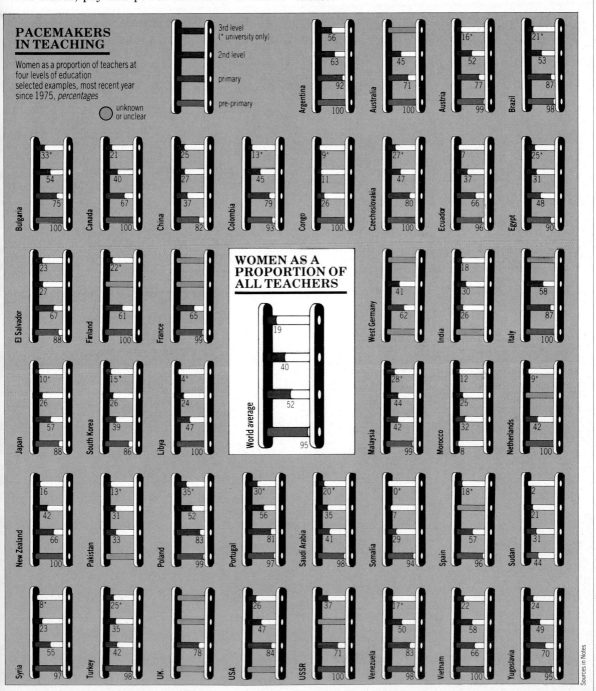

PACEMAKERS IN TEACHING

Women as a proportion of teachers at four levels of education selected examples, most recent year since 1975, *percentages*

3rd level (* university only)
2nd level
primary
pre-primary

○ unknown or unclear

WOMEN AS A PROPORTION OF ALL TEACHERS

World average: 19, 40, 52, 95

FEMINIST VOICES

Countries with feminist media and media services, 1985

● periodicals ■ presses publishers ● bookstores ↑ news services ■ radio television ▬ film/video /cable

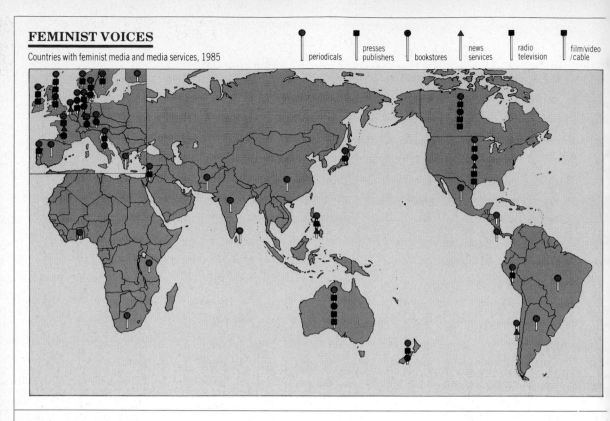

MEDIA WORKERS

Women as a proportion of workers in the media where known, most recent year since 1970s, *percentages*

■ women in all media
■ women in broadcast management
■ women in print media

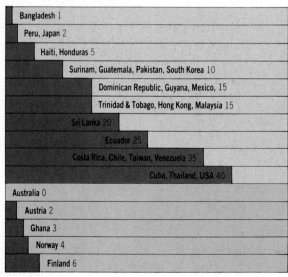

Bangladesh 1
Peru, Japan 2
Haiti, Honduras 5
Surinam, Guatemala, Pakistan, South Korea 10
Dominican Republic, Guyana, Mexico, 15
Trinidad & Tobago, Hong Kong, Malaysia 15
Sri Lanka 20
Ecuador 25
Costa Rica, Chile, Taiwan, Venezuela 35
Cuba, Thailand, USA 40
Australia 0
Austria 2
Ghana 3
Norway 4
Finland 6

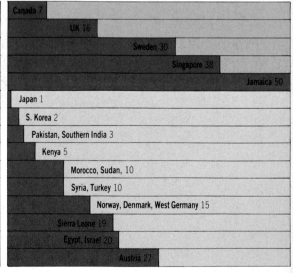

Canada 7
UK 16
Sweden 30
Singapore 38
Jamaica 50
Japan 1
S. Korea 2
Pakistan, Southern India 3
Kenya 5
Morocco, Sudan, 10
Syria, Turkey 10
Norway, Denmark, West Germany 15
Sierra Leone 19
Egypt, Israel 20
Austria 27

UP FRONT

Front-page stories written by women, USA, 1985, *percentages*

USA Today	41.5	Detroit Free Press	26.2	Philadelphia Inquirer	18.4
Boston Globe	30.5	Cleveland Plain Dealer	22.6	Los Angeles Times	17.7
Atlanta Journal	30.1	Chicago Tribune	19.2	New York Times	10.0
Washington Post	26.3	Wall Street Journal	18.8		

Radio, television, newspapers and magazines entertain and educate. They are also important means for maintaining or changing the status quo. The mass media are growing rapidly, but small media are flourishing, too. Mass media means male media.

Women's media image is predominantly passive, domestic and, especially in advertisements, sexual. Women's news is considered to be fashion, style, social trends. Women do not appear to make the news, either as features or writers. Women working in the media are predominantly in low-paid, low-status jobs.

There is a growing feminist media addressing the concerns of women worldwide, but it is small compared to the reach of traditional women's media. Most pervasive of all are the sex magazines for men: a highly profitable industry selling a perverse, widely accepted image of women.

THE FURTHEST REACH

Circulation by place of publication of selected magazines, mid-1980s, *thousands*

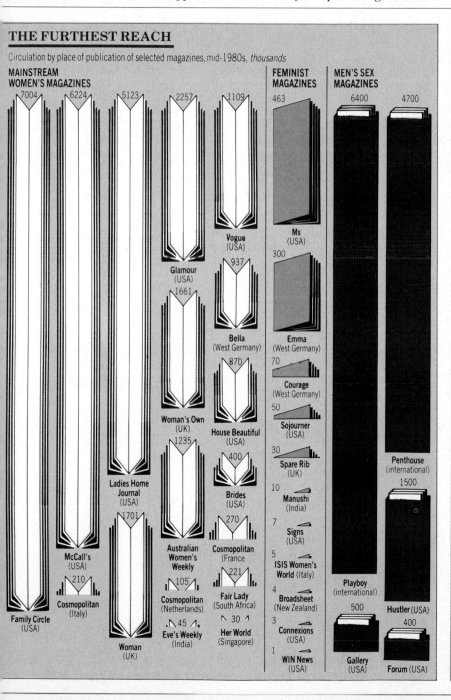

MAINSTREAM WOMEN'S MAGAZINES

7004 — Family Circle (USA)
6224 — McCall's (USA)
210 — Cosmopolitan (Italy)
5123 — Ladies Home Journal (USA)
1701 — Woman (UK)
2257 — Glamour (USA)
1661 — Woman's Own (UK)
1235 — Australian Women's Weekly
105 — Cosmopolitan (Netherlands)
45 — Eve's Weekly (India)
1109 — Vogue (USA)
937 — Bella (West Germany)
870 — House Beautiful (USA)
400 — Brides (USA)
270 — Cosmopolitan (France)
221 — Fair Lady (South Africa)
30 — Her World (Singapore)

FEMINIST MAGAZINES

463 — Ms (USA)
300 — Emma (West Germany)
70 — Courage (West Germany)
50 — Sojourner (USA)
30 — Spare Rib (UK)
10 — Manushi (India)
7 — Signs (USA)
5 — ISIS Women's World (Italy)
4 — Broadsheet (New Zealand)
3 — Connexions (USA)
1 — WIN News (USA)

MEN'S SEX MAGAZINES

6400 — Playboy (international)
500 — Gallery (USA)
4700 — Penthouse (international)
1500 — Hustler (USA)
400 — Forum (USA)

FANTASY WORLD

Circulation of Playboy, all editions, 1985–86, *thousands*

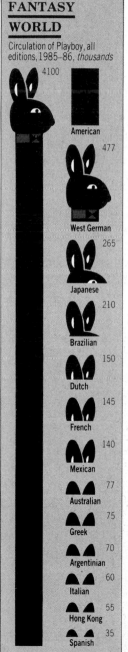

4100 — American
477 — West German
265 — Japanese
210 — Brazilian
150 — Dutch
145 — French
140 — Mexican
77 — Australian
75 — Greek
70 — Argentinian
60 — Italian
55 — Hong Kong
35 — Spanish

Sources in Notes

BODY BEAUTIFUL

Women's cosmetic surgery and percentage increase, USA, 1981-84

number of operations, 1984 | percentage increase since 1981

eye changes	nose changes	face-lifts	dermabrasion	ear changes	breast enlargement	breast lift	tummy tuck	fat removal (suction)	surgical body conto...
59,120 / 31	56,400 / 30	43,200 / 39	18,800 / 38	10,560 / 15	95,000 / 32	16,200 / 26	20,900 / 37	55,900	16,000

GREENLAND

ICELAND 1985

1961 1956

NORWAY 1959 1962

FINLAND 1952 1975 1957 Finland

UNION OF SOVIET SOCIALIST REPUBLICS

1961 1964
1965 1983
United Kingdom
UNITED KINGDOM

DENMARK

1955 1966 1984
1951 1952 1977
Sweden

MONGOLIA

PORTUGAL 1974 1969 SPAIN

1953 1953

1973 Athens
1964
Lebanon 1971

CHINA

1976 Hong Kong

MOROCCO ALGERIA LIBYA EGYPT 1954 1976 Israel SAUDI ARABIA IRAN AFGHANISTAN

WESTERN SAHARA MAURITANIA MALI NIGER CHAD SUDAN PAKISTAN INDIA 1966 1965 THAILAND

CAPE VERDE SENEGAL GUINEA NIGERIA CAR ETHIOPIA SRI LANKA

ZAIRE KENYA TANZANIA ANGOLA ZAMBIA ZIMBABWE MADAGASCAR MALDIVES SINGAPORE MALAYSI

NAMIBIA BOTSWANA

SOUTH AFRICA 1978 1958 1974

THE BEAUTY BUSINESS

World cosmetic sales, 1984-85, $ billion

Avon	Revlon	L'Oreal	Shiseido
2.6	2.4	1.9	1.5

SOME NATIONAL BEAUTY CONTESTS

USA ● children
Miss America
Miss USA
Mrs America
Miss Nude America

Miss Black America
Miss Senior America
Miss Indian America
Miss Wheelchair America
Miss Deaf America

Miss America Teenager
Miss Teen All-American
Miss Lovely Legs
Face of the Eighties
Maid of Cotton
Miss Avocado
Little Miss Lovely ●

National Lollipop Queen
Most Beautiful Girl in the World
UK ● childr
Miss Look of Radiance
Look of the Eighties
Miss Pears
European Queen of Beauty

BEAUTY BEAT 35

he quest for beauty is used to exalt and to degrade
women, and as a distraction from reality. Presented
as entertainment it has been turned into a serious
preoccupation. Beauty contests attempt to create a
fantasy world where women are meant to be ogled
and men are polite voyeurs. These contests can be
seen as simply part of the pornography continuum.

International beauty contests promote the export
of culturally-specific notions of beauty that women
everywhere are expected to meet: mostly, a white,
European standard. The idea of women as beauty-
objects transcends economic and political differences: rich and poor countries, communist and cap-
italist, all participate in the beauty beat.

Beauty is big business. Beauty contests are very
profitable, and more are spawned each year. The
cosmetics market is enormous. The demand for
cosmetic surgery grows yearly.

BODY POLITICS

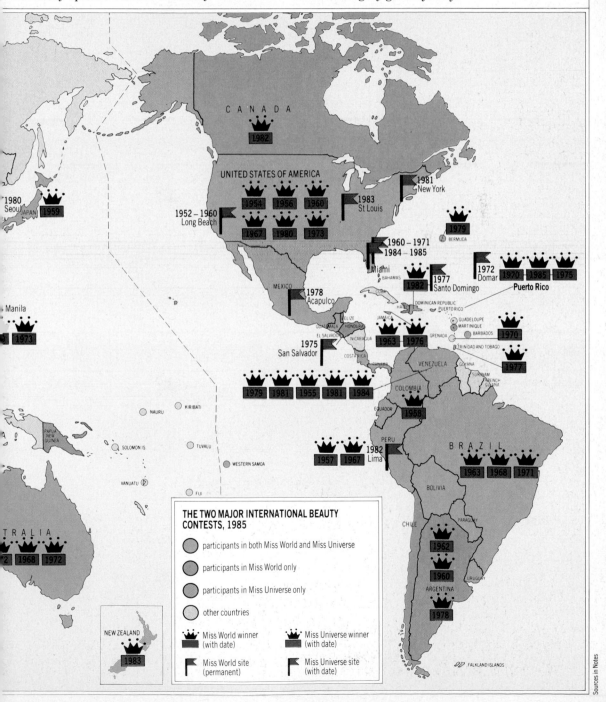

THE TWO MAJOR INTERNATIONAL BEAUTY
CONTESTS, 1985

- participants in both Miss World and Miss Universe
- participants in Miss World only
- participants in Miss Universe only
- other countries
- Miss World winner (with date)
- Miss Universe winner (with date)
- Miss World site (permanent)
- Miss Universe site (with date)

Sources in Notes

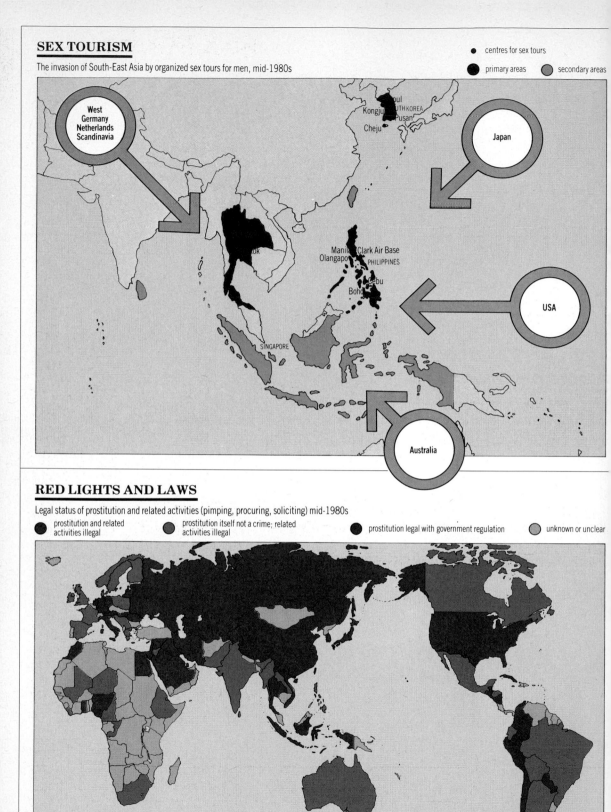

SEX TOURISM

The invasion of South-East Asia by organized sex tours for men, mid-1980s

- centres for sex tours
- primary areas
- secondary areas

West Germany Netherlands Scandinavia

Japan

USA

Australia

Seoul
Kongju SOUTH KOREA
Cheju Pusan

Manila Clark Air Base
Olangapo PHILIPPINES
Cebu
Bohol

SINGAPORE

RED LIGHTS AND LAWS

Legal status of prostitution and related activities (pimping, procuring, soliciting) mid-1980s

- prostitution and related activities illegal
- prostitution itself not a crime; related activities illegal
- prostitution legal with government regulation
- unknown or unclear

Prostitution is not a women's institution. It has always been controlled by men and sustained by violence. The image of the 'happy hooker' has little to do with reality. Poverty drives most women who 'choose' prostitution. Many girls are sold into prostitution by poor families. Once in the system, it is hard to get out.

In the international prostitution network, women are commodities. Prostitutes are traded, girls are bought and exchanged among pimps, marriage catalogues offer women for sale. Despite growing protests and exposure, the trade is flourishing and widespread.

Sex tours to South-East Asia for men represent an extreme of exploitation for women.

Prostitution exists in all countries, regardless of its legal status – but under different laws the treatment of prostitutes varies widely.

INTERNATIONAL TRAFFIC IN WOMEN

Women being bought, sold and traded, as determined by major cases exposed from the mid-1970s (internal trafficking not included)

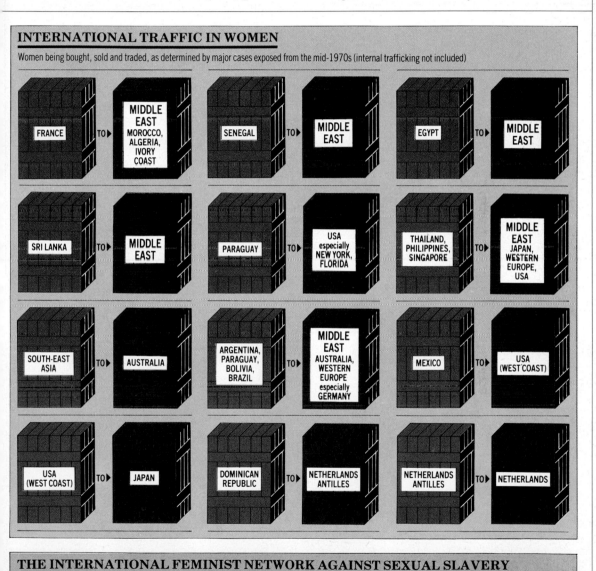

FRANCE TO▶ MIDDLE EAST MOROCCO, ALGERIA, IVORY COAST

SENEGAL TO▶ MIDDLE EAST

EGYPT TO▶ MIDDLE EAST

SRI LANKA TO▶ MIDDLE EAST

PARAGUAY TO▶ USA especially NEW YORK, FLORIDA

THAILAND, PHILIPPINES, SINGAPORE TO▶ MIDDLE EAST JAPAN, WESTERN EUROPE, USA

SOUTH-EAST ASIA TO▶ AUSTRALIA

ARGENTINA, PARAGUAY, BOLIVIA, BRAZIL TO▶ MIDDLE EAST AUSTRALIA, WESTERN EUROPE especially GERMANY

MEXICO TO▶ USA (WEST COAST)

USA (WEST COAST) TO▶ JAPAN

DOMINICAN REPUBLIC TO▶ NETHERLANDS ANTILLES

NETHERLANDS ANTILLES TO▶ NETHERLANDS

THE INTERNATIONAL FEMINIST NETWORK AGAINST SEXUAL SLAVERY

Countries with active participants, 1983

Australia	France	Netherlands Antilles	Tahiti
Brazil	West Germany	Peru	Thailand
Cameroon	India	Philippines	USA
Colombia	Japan	Sri Lanka	Zimbabwe
Dominican Republic	Lebanon	Sweden	
Egypt	Netherlands	Switzerland	

Sources in Notes

SEX AND RAPE OFFENCES

Officially reported rape and sex offences, number per 100,000 population, mid-1970s

○	5 and below
◔	5.1-15
◑	15.1-35
●	35.1-90
○	unclear or unknown

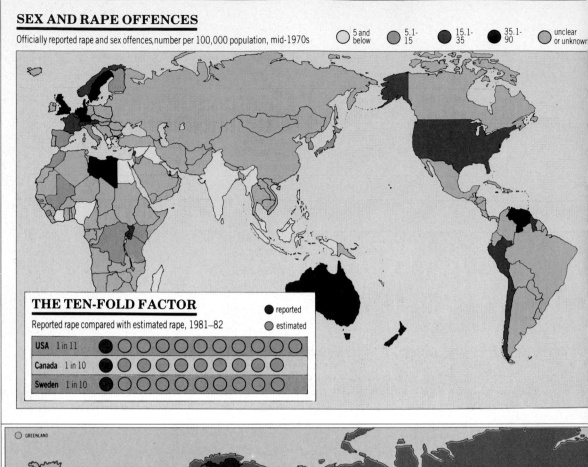

THE TEN-FOLD FACTOR

Reported rape compared with estimated rape, 1981–82

● reported
● estimated

USA	1 in 11	● ○○○○○○○○○○ ○	
Canada	1 in 10	● ○○○○○○○○○ ○	
Sweden	1 in 10	● ○○○○○○○○○ ○	

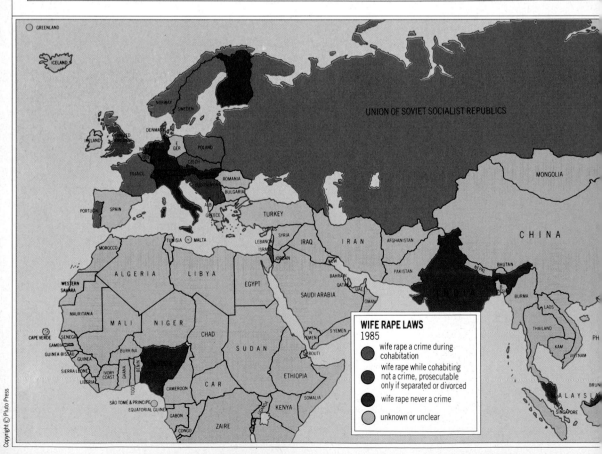

GREENLAND

ICELAND

NORWAY

SWEDEN

DENMARK

UNITED KINGDOM

IRELAND

NETH

BEL GER

FRANCE

POLAND

CZECH

ROMANIA

BULGARIA

YUGOSLAVIA

ALB

GREECE

UNION OF SOVIET SOCIALIST REPUBLICS

MONGOLIA

PORTUGAL SPAIN

ITALY

TUNISIA MALTA

TURKEY

CYPRUS

LEBANON SYRIA

ISRAEL

JORDAN

IRAQ

IRAN

AFGHANISTAN

CHINA

MOROCCO

WESTERN SAHARA

ALGERIA

LIBYA

EGYPT

SAUDI ARABIA

BAHRAIN

QATAR

UAE

OMAN

NEPAL

BHUTAN

BURMA

MAURITANIA

MALI

NIGER

CHAD

SUDAN

LAOS

THAILAND

CAPE VERDE

SENEGAL

GAMBIA

GUINEA BISSAU

GUINEA

SIERRA LEONE

LIBERIA

IVORY COAST

BURKINA

GHANA

TOGO

BENIN

NIGERIA

CAMEROON

CAR

ETHIOPIA

SOMALIA

N YEMEN

S YEMEN

DJIBOUTI

PAKISTAN

KAM

VIETNAM

PH

SÃO TOMÉ & PRINCIPE

EQUATORIAL GUINEA

GABON

CONGO

ZAIRE

UGANDA

KENYA

MALAYSIA

SINGAPORE

BRUN

WIFE RAPE LAWS
1985

●	wife rape a crime during cohabitation
●	wife rape while cohabiting not a crime, prosecutable only if separated or divorced
●	wife rape never a crime
○	unknown or unclear

Rape is probably the most under-reported, fastest growing and least convicted crime in the world. It has long been considered as only a crime against property – the woman as man's property. Now it is beginning to be recognized for what it is: a crime of violence and power, and a violation of women's civil rights.

Men of all ages and backgrounds rape women of all ages and backgrounds. Women everywhere live under the threat of rape, especially in their own homes. Rape in families is not a secret any more: wife-rape is now prosecutable in parts of Europe and the USA, and is slowly being recognized as a crime elsewhere. Grass-roots organizing by women has brought about these legal and social changes, including the setting up of rape-crisis centres.

But in most countries, rape is still not properly recognized as a serious problem for women.

OUT OF THE SHADOWS

Growth in the number of rape crisis centres

Increase in reported rapes, where known, *percentages*

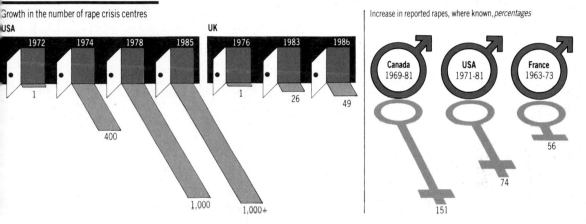

USA

1972	1974	1978	1985
1			
		400	
			1,000

UK

1976	1983	1986
1	26	49
		1,000+

Canada 1969-81 — 151

USA 1971-81 — 74

France 1963-73 — 56

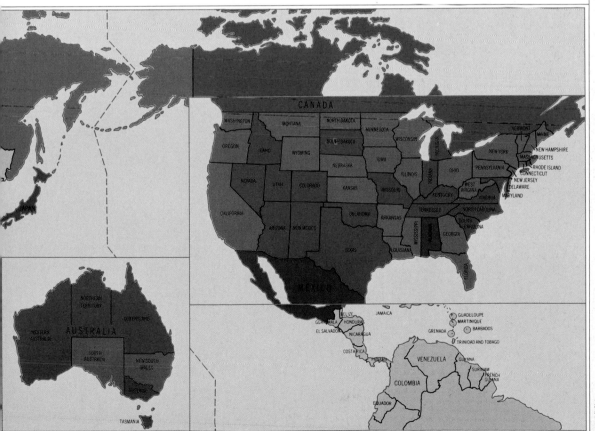

The women's movement has affected government and bureaucratic machinery internationally. Agendas now routinely include women's issues, and policy-making groups have women's advisory boards. These changes are often made reluctantly and may be primarily symbolic, but they are steps towards some improvement of women's status.

Ironically, channels of change for women are often not run by women. In most cases, women are barely represented in policy-making posts in governments or agencies, even those dealing mostly with women's issues.

Often the most effective channels are those that women set up themselves. Organizing by women is not new, but has certainly accelerated in the past decade. Conferences, international networks, non-government organizations and political action groups are at the forefront of change.

WOMEN ON THE INSIDE

Position of women workers in three international agencies, *percentages*

women   men

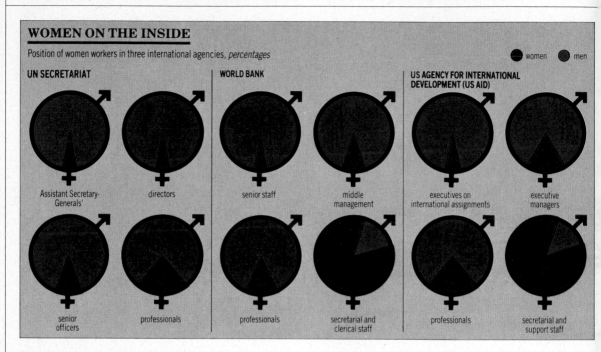

| UN SECRETARIAT | WORLD BANK | US AGENCY FOR INTERNATIONAL DEVELOPMENT (US AID) |

Assistant Secretary-Generals' · directors · senior staff · middle management · executives on international assignments · executive managers

senior officers · professionals · professionals · secretarial and clerical staff · professionals · secretarial and support staff

CONFERENCES

Representation of women by women in major international forums

UN CONFERENCE ON POPULATION
Mexico City, 1984

> 'improving the status of women may be the most effective and efficient solution to the population crisis... The formulation of population policy should include the full participation of women'
> *quote from the platform*

- of 140 countries represented, one-third had no women delegates
- the 18 dignitaries in the opening platform party were all men
- only 16 countries had women-headed delegations
- only one country, Western Samoa, had a women-majority delegation

INTERNATIONAL LABOR ORGANIZATION (ILO) ANNUAL CONFERENCES
The 1975 Annual Conference passed a resolution of equality of opportunity between men and women.
Women delegates/advisors to ILO conferences, *percentages*

1975	11	1980	11
1976	10	1981	10
1977	9	1982	9
1978	5	1983	10
1979	7	1984	9

UN DECADE FOR WOMEN CONFERENCE, 1985
- one-third of the delegates were men
- 14 of the country delegations were headed by men
- one delegation (North Korea) consisted entirely of men

GETTING TOGETHER

Women's international organizations and founding dates, selected examples

1880-1901	World Women's Christian Temperance Union International Council of Nurses General Federation of Women's Clubs
1900-1915	International Council of Jewish Women International Alliance of Women Women's International League for Peace and Freedom International Federation for Home Economics
1916-1930	Associated Country Women of the World International Conference of Midwives International Federation of Business and Professional Women International Federation of University Women Medical Women's International Association Zonta International
1931-1945	International Federation of Women Lawyers Women's International Democratic Federation
1946-1970	All African Women's Conference Federation of Asian Women's Associations International Union of Women Architects World Movement of Mothers
1970-1985	Arab Women Solidarity Association International Women's Studies Association International Network Against Female Sexual Slavery Conference of Non-Governmental Organizations

GOVERNMENT CHANNELS

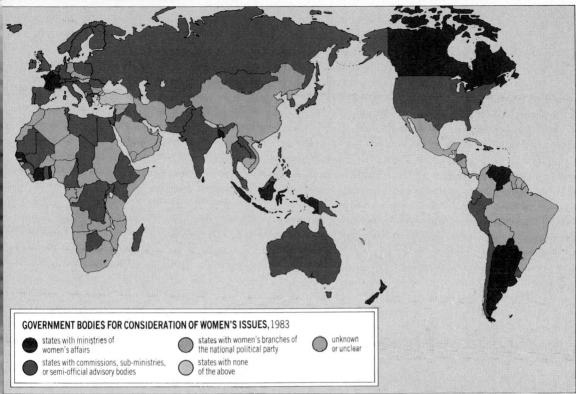

GOVERNMENT BODIES FOR CONSIDERATION OF WOMEN'S ISSUES, 1983

- states with ministries of women's affairs
- states with commissions, sub-ministries, or semi-official advisory bodies
- states with women's branches of the national political party
- states with none of the above
- unknown or unclear

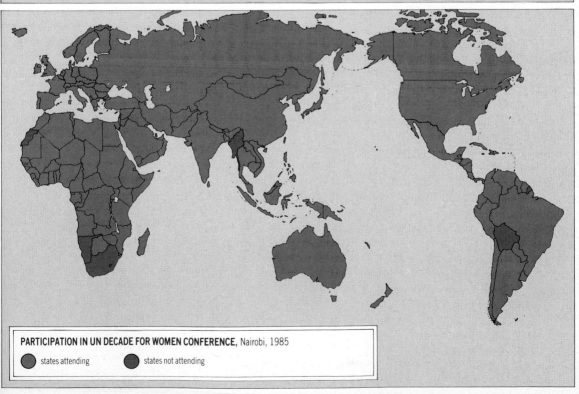

PARTICIPATION IN UN DECADE FOR WOMEN CONFERENCE, Nairobi, 1985

- states attending
- states not attending

Sources in Notes

EVERY DAY STRUGGLES   Other forms of women's protest

CONTRACEPTIVES MANUFACTURER FACES LEGAL CHARGES . . . . . .
WOMEN'S MARCH FOR PEACE . . . . . WOMEN PROTEST PORNOGRAPHY
FILM . . . . . . WOMEN PRESS CHARGES OF SEXUAL HARRASSMENT . .
SARI SQUAD PROTESTS DEPORTATION . . . . NURSES ON STRIKE . . .
WOMEN PROTEST DAYCARE CUTBACKS . . . TEXTILE WORKERS WALK OUT

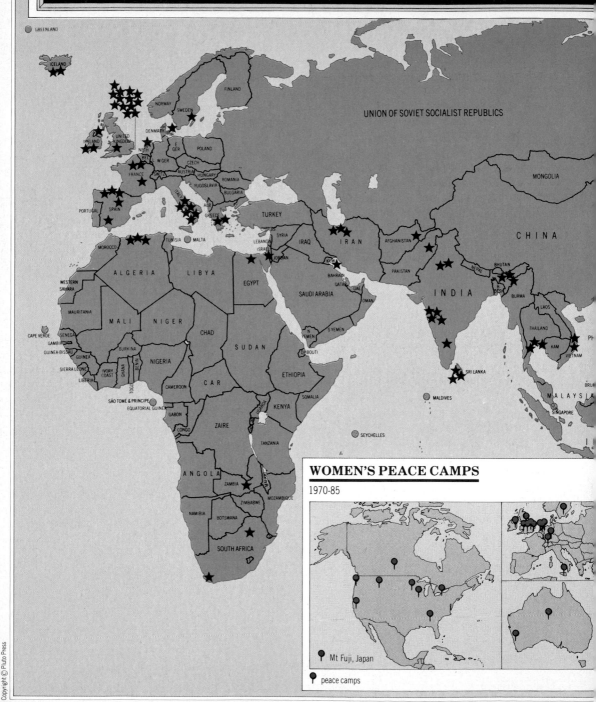

WOMEN'S PEACE CAMPS

1970-85

Mt Fuji, Japan

♀ peace camps

Women engage in many forms of protest: by challenging conventions in their marriages and workplaces; by opening battered women's refuges and women's bookstores; by starting alternative healthcare networks. Sometimes they take to the streets to make their voices heard on issues of violence, pornography, abortion, social security and peace.

Nowhere is there much support for women, as such, to organize. In many countries, a women's protest is in itself a major breakthrough, and flouts conventions of how women are supposed to behave. But almost all the advances in women's rights in the last century have been won only because women have been active on their own behalf.

Peace has always been a women's issue: women have been in the lead in anti-war and anti-militarist movements for the last century, as in the current women's peace camp movement.

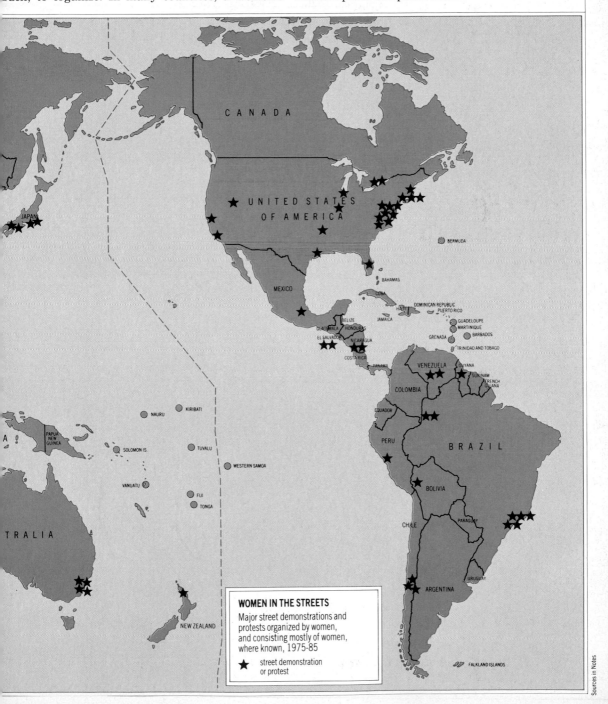

WOMEN IN THE STREETS

Major street demonstrations and protests organized by women, and consisting mostly of women, where known, 1975-85

★ street demonstration or protest

Sources in Notes

When official international agencies such as the United Nations gather statistics, they choose the subjects they consider important and accessible.

The statistics that exist on women reflect those choices. Information about women's fertility and use of contraceptives is considered critical, but data on maternal mortality is not. Similarly, conventional labour force statistics on women are systematically gathered, but data on women's unpaid labour is collected only sporadically. The 'official' woman is thus an incomplete one. Many aspects of her life are invisible including domestic violence, rape and poverty. Feminists and their organizations are still virtually the only sources for this officially unimportant information. Even when governments and agencies have the opportunity to collect or publish gender-specific data they sometimes choose not to.

Men in power still ignore women in numbers.

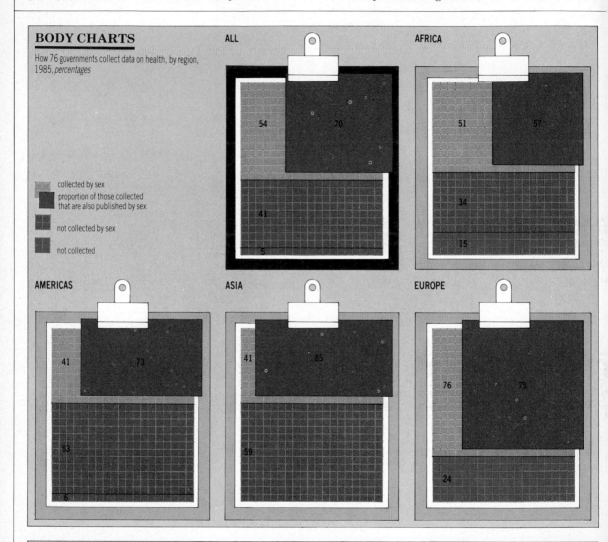

BODY CHARTS

How 76 governments collect data on health, by region, 1985, *percentages*

ALL

AFRICA

54   70

51   57

41

34

5

15

collected by sex

proportion of those collected that are also published by sex

not collected by sex

not collected

AMERICAS

ASIA

EUROPE

41   73

41   85

76   75

53

59

24

6

INVISIBLE WOMEN

Parts of women's lives not recorded in the standard international sources, mid-1980s

child marriage	see map 2	time use and the division of labour	see map 13	military service	see map 32
domestic violence	3	migration for work	17	media	34
genital mutilation	4	job ghettos	18	beauty contests	35
polygyny	5	land rights	21	sexual slavery and prostitution	36
reproductive technology	6	university admissions	23	rape and wife rape	37
sterilization abuse	7	women refugees	27	women's organizations	38
illegal abortion and attacks on abortion	9	feminization of poverty	28	protests	39

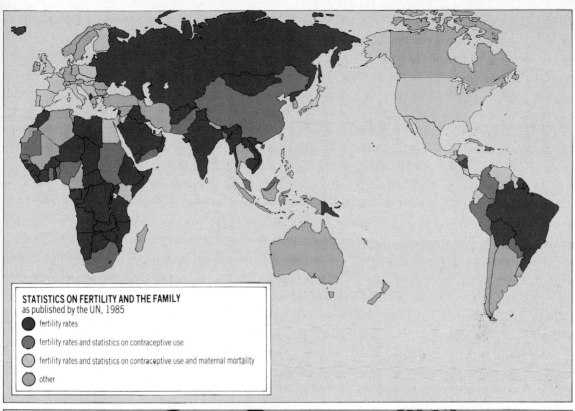

STATISTICS ON FERTILITY AND THE FAMILY
as published by the UN, 1985

- fertility rates
- fertility rates and statistics on contraceptive use
- fertility rates and statistics on contraceptive use and maternal mortality
- other

STATISTICS ON WORK AND WORKERS
as published by the UN, 1985

- women in waged work
- women in waged work and in unpaid labour
- women in waged work, and statistics on wages
- women in waged work, in unpaid labour and statistics on wages
- other

	Population 000s 1985		Rural population percentages 1980		Population over 60 years percentages 1980		Marriage minimum legal age with parental consent		Children per mother average number	Contracept[...] use by women percentages
	F	M	F	M	F	M	F	M		
Afghanistan	7141	7495	42	43	4	4	16	18	6.9	2
Albania	1505	1545	32	31	8	6	NA		NA	NA
Algeria	11000	11000	20	20	6	5	16	18	7.0	<15
Angola	4448	4306	42	37	5	5	NA		6.5	1
Antigua and Barbuda	34	31	NA		10	6	NA		2.5	NA
Argentina	15400	15200	8	10	14	11	16	18	3.4	40–59
Australia	7835	7879	5	6	16	13	16	18	2.1	72
Austria	3920	3567	23	22	24	15	16	19	1.6	>60
Bahamas	106	104	NA		7	6	NA		2.5	NA
Bahrain	177	254	11	11	4	3	NA		5.2	<15
Bangladesh	49000	52100	43	45	5	5	16	18	6.6	12
Barbados	138	127	31	30	15	11	16	16	2.6	30
Belgium	5032	4848	14	14	22	17	15	18	1.6	76
Belize	60	60	NA		7	6	NA		4.5	<15
Benin	2038	1967	35	34	5	4	None		7.0	1
Bermuda	NA		NA		NA		NA		NA	NA
Bhutan	686	731	47	49	6	5	NA		6.1	<15
Bolivia	3232	3139	34	33	6	5	12	14	6.8	<15
Botswana	564	515	39	32	4	3	NA		6.5	8
Brazil	67900	67700	16	17	7	6	16	18	4.2	40–59
Brunei	93	107	NA		4	4	NA		NA	15–39
Bulgaria	4637	4583	18	18	19	16	18	18	2.2	40–59
Burkina	3507	3432	46	45	5	4	NA		6.5	1
Burma	19800	19700	37	36	6	6	NA		5.5	<15
Burundi	2372	2260	50	48	6	5	NA		6.5	1
Cameroon	4932	4782	34	31	7	6	15	18	6.4	1
Canada	12900	12700	12	13	15	12	16	16	1.8	68
Cape Verde	162	159	48	47	7	6	NA		3.0	NA
CAR	1324	1243	31	28	7	5	16	18	5.9	<15
Chad	2547	2472	42	40	6	5	NA		5.9	1
Chile	6096	5979	9	10	9	7	12	14	3.1	43
China	521000	542000	37	38	9	7	20	22	2.3	70
Colombia	14300	14400	14	16	6	5	14	16	3.6	52
Comoros	231	226	45	43	5	4	NA		6.2	NA
Congo	882	858	33	30	6	5	NA		5.9	<15
Costa Rica	1287	1313	27	30	6	5	15	15	3.7	64
Cuba	4925	5113	16	19	11	11	14	16	2.1	40–59
Cyprus	334	333	27	26	15	13	16	18	2.3	NA
Czechoslovakia	7996	7652	19	18	19	14	18	18	2.3	66
Denmark	2608	2536	7	8	22	18	18	18	1.5	67
Djibouti	NA		NA		NA		NA		NA	<15
Dominica	NA		NA		NA		NA		3.4	NA
Dominican Republic	3101	3142	23	26	5	5	15	16	4.2	43

Maternal mortality deaths per 100,000 live births	Proportion of women in labour force percentages	Labour force percentages		Agricultural labour force percentages		Proportion of girls in secondary education percentages	Illiteracy percentages		Life expectancy at birth years		Anaemia during pregnancy percentages	Right to vote won by women year
		F	M	F	M		F	M	F	M		
	21	18	88	3	97	4	94	67	37.3	36.6	NA	1964
	59	40	60	50	50	60	NA		71.5	68	NA	1946
	7	9	91	5	95	29	87	58	56.3	54.4	65	1958
3	9	9	91	47	53	6	NA		41.6	38.5	NA	1975
	29	NA		NA		NA	NA		NA		NA	1951
	29	27	73	4	96	60	8	7	72.1	65.4	61	1947
	48	38	62	24	76	88	0	0	77	70.1	NA	1902
	49	39	61	48	52	76	<1	<1	75.6	68.5	NA	1919
	34	NA		NA		79	<10	<10	NA		NA	1962
	15	11	89	NA		52	30	15	68.1	64.1	NA	
	13	17	83	4	69	6	87	63	46.1	47.1	66	1956
	63	46	54	48	52	85	<1	<1	73.2	67.9	NA	1951
	48	37	63	26	74	89	<1	<1	75.7	69.1	NA	1948
	NA	NA		NA		NA	9	9	NA		NA	1954
	40	36	64	21	79	8	83	60	42.1	39.0	NA	1956
	72	45	55	NA		NA	1	2	NA		NA	1944
	NA	NA		40	60	5	NA		43.1	44.6	NA	
	22	22	78	27	73	31	49	24	50.9	46.5	NA	1952
	44	40	60	95	5	23	56	63	54.2	50.8	NA	1966
	29	27	73	15	85	35	26	22	64.3	59.5	20	1932
	27	24	76	28	72	NA	50	25	NA		NA	NA
	67	43	57	58	42	83	8	3	73.8	68.7	NA	1947
	81	43	57	46	54	2	97	85	41.6	38.5	NA	1956
	46	36	64	25	75	18	44	24	54.1	51	55	1935
	95	53	47	56	44	2	85	61	43.6	40.4	NA	1961
	52	38	62	92	8	12	76	45	47.6	44.4	NA	1956
	56	41	59	25	75	90	0	0	78.1	70.5	NA	1920
4	NA	NA		19	81	NA	NA		56.2	53.1	42	1975
	83	48	52	52	48	7	81	52	42.6	39.4	NA	1956
	28	24	76	27	73	1	99	64	42.6	39.4	NA	1956
	30	30	70	4	96	59	12	10	69	62.4	32	1949
	55	36	64	47	53	27	37	14	66.5	62.6	NA	1947
4	27	38	62	14	86	49	20	18	64.5	60	22	1957
	NA	NA		34	66	17	48	34	49.7	46.4	NA	NA
	43	37	63	34	66	53	49	25	46.1	43	NA	1956
	25	25	75	5	95	51	12	11	74	69	44	1949
	36	31	69	15	85	77	5	4	74.4	71.1	NA	1934
	46	39	61	59	41	66	17	4	75.5	72	NA	1959
	71	47	53	42	58	56	0	0	74.1	67	NA	1919
	72	45	55	24	76	85	0	0	77.3	71.3	NA	1915
	NA	NA		NA		NA	NA		NA		NA	1957
5	NA	37	63	27	73	NA	6	6	NA		46	1967
	13	12	88	44	54	33	34	31	62.2	58.4	NA	1942

	Population 000s 1985		Rural population percentages 1980		Population over 60 years percentages 1980		Marriage minimum legal age with parental consent		Children per mother average number	Contracept use by women percentages
	F	M	F	M	F	M	F	M		
Ecuador	4682	4698	27	29	5	5	12	14	6.3	6
Egypt	23000	23800	27	27	7	6	16	18	5.3	20
El Salvador	2764	2788	28	30	6	5	14	16	5.8	34
Equatorial Guinea	200	192	25	21	7	6	NA		5.7	<15
Ethiopia	18300	18200	44	41	4	4	var.		6.5	1
Fiji	342	343	28	29	6	6	16	18	3.6	40
Finland	2518	2357	19	19	21	13	17	18	1.6	77
France	27800	26800	11	11	20	15	15	18	1.8	82
French Guiana	NA		NA		NA		NA		NA	NA
French Polynesia	55	58	NA		4	5	NA		NA	NA
Gabon	593	574	34	30	10	9	15	18	4.4	<15
The Gambia	326	317	41	40	5	5	None		6.4	1
Germany, East	8771	7871	12	11	24	14	18	18	1.8	>60
Germany, West	31700	29400	7	8	24	15	16	16	1.4	>60
Ghana	6804	6674	33	32	5	4	None	21	6.5	4
Greece	5049	4884	19	19	20	16	14	18	2.3	>60
Greenland	NA		NA		NA		NA		NA	>60
Grenada	NA		NA		NA		16	16	NA	NA
Guadeloupe	164	156	28	29	12	10	15	18	3.0	44
Guatemala	4143	4260	29	32	5	5	14	16	5.7	19
Guinea	2747	2683	41	40	5	5	17	18	6.5	1
Guinea–Bissau	458	432	38	38	7	6	NA		5.4	1
Guyana	476	478	39	40	6	6	14	16	3.9	31
Haiti	3337	3248	37	38	6	5	None		4.6	5
Honduras	2181	2192	31	33	5	4	12	14	6.5	9
Hong Kong	2665	2944	5	5	13	10	16	16	2.1	72
Hungary	5552	5245	23	23	21	15	14	16	2.1	73
Iceland	119	123	5	6	15	12	18	18	2.3	>60
India	367000	394000	38	40	6	6	18	21	5.0	16
Indonesia	82800	82100	40	39	6	5	16	19	4.8	26
Iran	22100	23000	25	25	5	5	NA		6.0	24
Iraq	7725	7951	14	14	5	4	18	18	7.0	23
Ireland	1795	1800	20	22	16	13	16	16	3.5	60
Israel	2146	2152	5	6	13	11	None	16	3.5	40–59
Italy	29000	27800	15	15	21	17	16	18	1.9	>60
Ivory Coast	4792	5006	31	31	5	5	15	18	6.7	<15
Jamaica	1171	1152	29	30	9	8	16	16	3.9	38
Japan	61000	59100	11	11	16	12	16	18	1.9	65
Jordan	1699	1811	22	22	4	4	17	18	7.2	22
Kampuchea	3717	3677	43	43	5	4	NA		4.1	NA
Kenya	10300	10300	44	41	3	3	var.		8.2	7
Korea, North	10100	10000	20	20	7	5	NA		4.5	NA
Korea, South	20300	20600	22	23	8	6	16	18	3.5	50

Maternal mortality deaths per 10,000 live births	Proportion of women in labour force percentages	Labour force percentages		Agricultural labour force percentages		Proportion of girls in secondary education percentages	Illiteracy percentages		Life expectancy at birth years		Anaemia during pregnancy percentages	Right to vote won by women year
		F	M	F	M		F	M	F	M		
2	19	21	79	12	88	42	30	22	62	58	NA	1929
	7	11	89	8	92	39	78	46	55.6	53.9	75	1956
	42	35	65	23	77	23	41	35	64.5	60	15	1950
A	4	5	95	3	97	4	NA		43.6	40.4	NA	
A	56	39	61	34	66	8	99	92	42.5	39.3	6	1955
	13	13	87	8	92	64	20	16	73.1	69.5	68	1962
	63	47	53	37	63	95	0	0	76.6	68	NA	1906
	53	40	60	30	70	89	0	0	78	69.8	NA	1944
	55	NA		NA		NA	NA		NA		NA	NA
A	NA	NA		NA		NA	NA		NA		NA	NA
A	54	NA		44	56	23	45	28	48.7	45.4	NA	1956
A	71	44	56	49	51	8	88	71	35	32	80	1961
	72	46	56	43	57	84	0	0	74.6	68.8	NA	1919
	50	39	61	48	52	90	0	0	75.8	69	NA	1919
A	56	42	58	54	46	27	82	57	51.7	48.3	64	1955
	34	31	69	40	60	76	24	7	75	71.3	NA	1952
A	NA	NA		NA		NA	NA		NA		NA	1915
	NA	38	92	NA		NA	2	2	NA		NA	1967
	53	43	57	22	78	NA	NA		71.8	66.5	NA	1944
2	13	15	85	6	94	15	62	46	58.8	56.9	34	1965
A	59	41	59	44	56	9	96	66	39.8	36.7	NA	1956
A	2	4	86	2	98	7	87	75	42.6	39.4	85	1973
4	26	25	75	10	90	61	11	6	68.9	64.1	55	1966
A	54	41	59	53	47	12	83	74	52.2	49.1	NA	1950
A	17	17	83	7	93	30	45	41	58.9	55.4	NA	1955
	49	36	64	26	74	65	36	10	NA		NA	
	59	43	57	36	64	47	2	1	73.3	66.7	NA	1945
	38	30	70	12	88	77	NA		79.3	73.4	NA	1915
A	30	26	74	24	76	20	81	52	50	51.2	68	1949
A	39	33	67	33	67	22	55	31	51.3	48.7	65	1945
A	14	14	86	12	88	32	76	52	58	58.4	50	1963
A	4	4	96	37	63	38	77	37	60.9	57.2	NA	1964
	34	30	70	10	90	98	7	4	74.6	69.6	NA	1922
	38	37	63	19	81	78	17	7	74.9	71.4	29	1948
	39	34	66	36	64	71	7	5	76.9	70.4	NA	1945
A	75	41	59	81	19	8	76	55	49.6	43.4	34	1956
6	75	46	54	18	82	60	4	4	71	67	24	1944
	54	38	62	48	52	92	<1	<1	78.3	73.1	NA	1945
	6	7	93	1	99	66	46	19	62	58.3	NA	1982
A	NA	NA		NA		NA	77	26	32.5	30	NA	1956
4	44	34	66	18	82	80	65	40	52.3	48.9	48	1963
A	69	46	54	56	44	NA	NA		64.6	60.5	NA	1946
A	48	39	61	44	56	80	19	6	68.8	62.4	NA	1946

	Population 000s 1985		Rural population percentages 1980		Population over 60 years percentages 1980		Marriage minimum legal age with parental consent		Children per mother average number	Contracept use by women percentages
	F	M	F	M	F	M	F	M		
Kuwait	748	1038	6	6	3	3	None		6.2	<15
Laos	2195	2228	43	43	5	5	NA		6.1	NA
Lebanon	1379	1289	12	12	8	8	var.		3.8	57
Lesotho	783	736	48	48	6	5	16	18	5.8	5
Liberia	1105	1086	35	33	5	5	16	16	6.9	1
Libya	1705	1900	23	25	4	4	var.		7.2	<15
Luxembourg	183	179	11	11	22	16	15	18	1.5	>60
Macau	121	128	NA		8	6	NA		NA	NA
Madagascar	5045	4967	42	40	6	5	14	17	6.5	<15
Malawi	3601	3415	35	31	4	4	NA		7.8	1
Malaysia	7711	7841	35	36	6	6	18	18	4.3	33
Maldives	68	75	NA		3	5	NA		NA	NA
Mali	4156	3897	41	39	5	4	15	18	6.7	1
Malta	199	183	8	8	15	12	14	16	2.0	NA
Martinique	161	152	16	17	13	11	15	18	2.6	51
Mauritania	954	935	32	32	5	4	NA		6.9	1
Mauritius	531	519	24	24	7	5	15	18	3.1	52
Mexico	39400	39600	16	17	6	5	14	16	5.4	40
Mongolia	948	952	25	25	6	5	NA		5.4	NA
Morocco	11800	11800	29	30	5	5	var.		6.1	7
Mozambique	7144	6942	47	45	6	5	NA		6.1	<15
Namibia	781	769	29	26	6	5	NA		6.1	<15
Nauru	NA		NA		NA		NA		NA	NA
Nepal	8030	8453	47	48	5	5	16	18	6.5	3
Netherlands	7296	7211	12	12	19	15	16	18	1.6	64
New Zealand	1645	1646	7	8	15	12	16	16	2.2	>60
Nicaragua	1636	1636	22	24	4	4	14	15	6.3	9
Niger	3086	3029	45	42	5	4	16	18	7.0	1
Nigeria	48100	47100	41	39	4	4	var.		7.1	<15
Norway	2092	2057	23	24	23	19	18	18	1.8	71
Oman	579	649	NA		4	4	NA		7.1	<15
Pakistan	48900	52800	35	37	4	4	16	18	6.4	5
Panama	1069	1112	21	24	7	7	16	18	3.5	54
Papua New Guinea	1768	1928	36	36	5	5	16	18	6.3	3
Paraguay	1844	1838	29	31	6	5	12	14	5.2	24
Peru	9744	9923	16	16	6	5	14	16	5.4	31
Philippines	27100	27600	31	33	5	5	14	16	4.6	37
Poland	19200	18400	22	22	16	11	16	16	2.3	57
Portugal	5281	4796	36	34	17	13	16	16	2.3	NA
Puerto Rico	1774	1683	16	14	12	11	NA		2.8	62
Qatar	102	199	NA		5	4	NA		6.8	<15
Reunion	280	283	22	24	6	7	NA		2.8	NA
Romania	11700	11400	26	26	16	12	16	18	2.4	40–59

Maternal mortality deaths per 1,000 live births	Proportion of women in labour force percentages	Labour force percentages		Agricultural labour force percentages		Proportion of girls in secondary education percentages	Illiteracy percentages		Life expectancy at birth years		Anaemia during pregnancy percentages	Right to vote won by women year
		F	M	F	M		F	M	F	M		
	19	13	87	1	99	70	66	35	71.6	66.9	NA	
	71	45	55	47	53	14	64	49	49	46.1	62	1956
	18	20	80	23	77	56	42	22	67	63.1	50	1957
	72	44	56	46	54	20	20	43	49	45.7	NA	1966
	39	31	69	88	12	11	88	70	48.7	45.4	NA	1946
	5	5	95	2	98	54	85	39	57	53.8	47	1963
	39	33	67	NA		66	0	0	75.7	68.2	NA	1918
	NA	NA		NA		NA	NA		NA		NA	NA
	74	45	55	91	9	10	NA		48.5	47	NA	1956
	54	37	63	96	4	2	81	53	44.6	41.4	49	1964
	40	34	66	38	62	51	55	28	67.1	63.5	77	1957
	64	37	63	NA		NA	18	18	NA		NA	NA
	17	17	83	91	9	5	94	87	41.6	38.5	50	1956
	22	24	76	12	88	63	18	12	73	68.4	NA	1947
	56	45	55	24	76	NA	NA		72.2	67.4	NA	1944
	4	4	96	NA		4	NA		43.6	40.4	24	1956
8	25	27	73	39	61	50	28	14	67.3	62.6	80	1958
9	21	20	80	9	91	49	20	12	66.3	61.9	38	1953
	43	33	67	36	64	92	NA		64.6	60.5	NA	1924
	14	16	84	25	75	18	90	66	57	53.8	46	1959
	85	52	48	35	65	4	77	56	49.1	45.8	NA	1975
	NA	NA		NA		NA	NA		47.5	45	NA	1966
	NA	NA		NA		NA	NA		NA		NA	1968
	45	35	65	39	61	9	95	67	43.1	44.6	33	1951
	39	34	66	15	85	91	0	0	78.6	72.1	NA	1919
	44	34	66	22	78	82	0	0	75.7	69.3	NA	1893
	25	22	78	8	92	47	43	42	57.3	55.3	20	1955
	11	10	90	11	89	2	94	86	42.1	39	57	1956
	53	40	60	35	65	6	77	55	48.1	44.9	65	1954
	66	41	59	31	69	95	0	0	78.6	72.2	NA	1913
	NA	NA		NA		7	NA		48.4	46.2	NA	
	11	12	88	3	97	8	90	70	47	49	65	1956
	27	30	70	5	95	69	13	13	70.9	67.6	NA	1946
	70	41	59	46	54	7	76	61	50	50.5	55	1975
0	22	20	80	14	86	26	25	15	66.4	61.9	NA	1961
8	26	25	75	21	79	52	38	17	58.8	55.2	35	1955
1	53	39	61	27	73	68	19	16	64.3	60.9	47	1937
	65	45	55	49	51	80	2	1	75	67	NA	1918
	51	41	59	50	50	56	35	22	72.9	66.1	NA	1975
	25	34	66	2	2	NA	13	11	77.1	70.3	NA	1936
	2	NA		NA		77	NA		71.6	66.7	NA	
	37	NA		4	96	NA	NA		66.7	63	NA	NA
5	66	46	54	50	50	72	0	0	72.2	67.5	NA	1948

	Population 000s 1985		Rural population percentages 1980		Population over 60 years percentages 1980		Marriage minimum legal age with parental consent		Children per mother average number	Contracept use by women percentages
	F	M	F	M	F	M	F	M		
Rwanda	3098	3017	49	47	5	4	NA		7.3	<15
St Christopher (St Kitts) – Nevis	24	22	NA		13	9	NA		3.6	NA
St Lucia	64	57	NA		9	6	NA		4.5	NA
St Vincent – Grenadines	NA		NA		NA		15	16	4.0	NA
Sao Tome and Principe	NA		NA		NA		NA		5.2	NA
Saudi Arabia	5104	6137	16	17	5	4	13	13	7.3	<15
Senegal	3293	3227	38	37	5	4	16	20	6.5	<15
Seychelles	32	32	NA		11	7	NA		4.2	NA
Sierra Leone	1837	1765	38	37	6	5	None		6.5	6
Singapore	1263	1309	12	14	8	7	18	18	1.8	71
Solomon Islands	102	111	NA		4	6	NA		NA	NA
Somalia	3011	2541	38	32	8	5	16	None	6.5	1
South Africa	16300	16100	27	23	7	6	16	18	5.1	<15
Spain	19900	19100	13	13	18	14	16	18	2.6	47
Sri Lanka	8054	8350	36	37	7	7	var.		3.9	32
Sudan	10700	10800	37	38	5	4	None		6.9	<15
Surinam	179	174	28	28	7	6	NA		4.6	15–39
Swaziland	332	317	46	45	5	4	16	18	6.5	<15
Sweden	4177	4102	6	7	25	21	18	18	1.7	75
Switzerland	3207	3083	21	21	27	17	18	20	1.5	>60
Syria	5203	5378	25	25	5	4			7.4	23
Taiwan	NA		NA		NA		NA		2.5	65
Tanzania	11400	11100	45	43	4	3	15	18	7.1	<15
Thailand	25700	25900	43	43	6	5	17	17	3.9	52
Togo	1481	1442	42	41	5	5	17	20	6.1	<15
Trinidad and Tobago	560	558	38	41	9	8	var.		3.1	44
Tunisia	3583	3926	24	24	6	7	17	20	5.6	19
Turkey	24300	25700	27	25	7	6	15	17	5.0	40
Uganda	7916	7782	45	43	4	4	16	18	7.0	<15
United Arab Emirates	411	901	NA		5	3	NA		6.8	<15
United Kingdom	28400	27200	5	5	23	17	16	16	1.8	71
Uruguay	1530	1483	7	9	17	14	NA		2.9	40–59
USA	122000	11600	11	12	18	14	var.		1.8	79
USSR	147000	13100	NA		NA		18	18	2.4	
Vanuatu	52	59	NA		4	5	NA		NA	NA
Venezuela	9194	9192	8	9	5	5	16	16	4.7	42
Vietnam	30500	28900	42	39	7	6	NA		5.5	NA
Yemen, North	1074	1051	33	30	5	4	NA		6.8	<15
Yemen, South	3448	3100	48	42	6	6	16	18	7.0	<15
Yugoslavia	11700	11400	29	29	15	11	18	18	2.0	59
Zaire	16800	16300	32	39	5	4	NA		6.1	1
Zambia	3354	3312	32	30	5	4	16	16	6.8	1
Zimbabwe	4423	4344	40	37	5	4	NA		8.0	14

A = not available

Maternal mortality deaths per 10,000 live births	Proportion of women in labour force percentages	Labour force percentages F	M	Agricultural labour force percentages F	M	Proportion of girls in secondary education percentages	Illiteracy percentages F	M	Life expectancy at birth years F	M	Anaemia during pregnancy percentages	Right to vote won by women year
A	94	52	48	56	44	1	61	39	49.2	45.9	NA	1962
	NA	38	62	NA		NA	2	2	NA		NA	1967
	NA	36	64	NA		NA	18	19	NA		NA	1967
	NA	34	66	NA		NA	5	4	NA		NA	1967
A	41	22	78	33	67	NA	NA		NA		NA	NA
A	5	5	95	33	67	24	88	66	54.6	51.5	NA	
A	66	42	58	60	40	7	94	67	42.9	39.7	NA	1956
A	49	38	62	24	56	NA	40	44	NA		NA	NA
A	43	35	65	61	39	8	91	70	33.5	30.6	45	1961
	38	35	65	23	77	58	26	8	73.1	68.6	26	1965
A	NA	NA		NA		NA	NA		NA		NA	NA
A	37	27	73	32	68	6	97	90	42.5	39.3	NA	1958
32	46	34	66	36	64	17	NA		53.2	49.8	25	
3	34	25	75	26	74	86	11	5	76.5	70.6	NA	1931
A	29	34	66	29	71	54	19	9	66.5	63.5	62	1934
A	12	11	89	21	79	12	94	64	46.4	43.9	NA	1965
A	NA	NA		21	79	51	37	32	70.2	65.5	NA	
A	71	46	54	49	51	40	47	43	49.5	42.9	NA	1968
	77	47	53	25	75	90	0	0	78.3	72.3	NA	1919
	50	36	64	26	74	57	NA		78.6	72	NA	1971
A	9	12	78	16	84	35	80	40	65.6	63.2	NA	1949
A	NA	NA		NA		NA	16	5	NA		NA	
A	78	51	49	98	2	3	30	22	50.7	47.3	59	1961
A	73	47	53	50	50	26	30	13	63.2	59.3	48	1932
A	54	42	58	33	67	16	93	73	48.2	45	47	1956
17	33	29	71	22	'78	57	10	5	71	66.5	56	1946
A	7	23	77	21	79	23	75	49	58.6	57.6	38	1959
A	44	34	66	87	13	24	47	17	62.8	58.3	74	1934
A	46	34	66	35	65	3	60	35	51.7	48.3	35	1962
A	NA	NA		3	97	57	62	42	71.6	66.7	NA	
0	54	40	60	19	81	84	0	0	76	69.7	NA	1928
4	35	38	62	4	64	65	6	7	73	66.4	NA	1932
2	56	43	57	20	80	95	<1	<1	77.2	69.4	NA	1920
A	58	51	49	44	56	121	<1	<1	74.3	65	NA	1917
A	NA	NA		NA		NA	NA		NA		NA	NA
5	29	27	73	3	97	42	27	20	69	63.6	52	1947
A	63	45	55	61	39	43	NA		58.1	53.7	NA	1956
A	4	5	95	30	70	15	99	82	45.1	43	NA	NA
A	5	6	94	4	96	2	92	52	42.2	40.4	NA	1970
5	47	39	61	42	58	80	24	8	72.9	67.6	NA	1946
A	60	43	57	52	48	13	63	26	49.7	46.4	NA	1960
A	41	32	68	39	61	11	42	21	51	47.7	60	1964
6	36	29	71	26	74	13	39	24	55.6	51.3	27	1980

1 WOMEN IN THE WORLD

This map introduces the general theme of the atlas as a whole: that while women represent more than half of the world's population, they nowhere share the same rights as men. Most of the specifics mapped in this atlas follow from this basic inequality.

The sex ratio shows the general demographic balance between men and women. It also gives information on the gendered geography of wars, migration and discrimination. Some of the countries where women greatly outnumber men reflect the loss of men in wars; others are countries with high rates of male out-migration. In the Arab Gulf states, women are greatly outnumbered by men because these countries have huge influxes of migrant male workers. But the general pattern showing where women are in the minority also reflects a more ominous influence: most of these are countries where women's status is very low. These are the countries where women work harder, die younger and die in childbirth, and where girl children are less valued.

There are many ways of summarizing women's status relative to men's. One is economic, and here the well-known United Nations quote from 1980 is still relevant: 'Women constitute half the world's population, perform nearly two-thirds of its work hours, receive one-tenth of the world's income, and own less than one-hundredth of the world's property.' Another indicator is women's legal status: nowhere in the world do women have the same legal or constitutional rights as men. The legal provision of rights does not guarantee 'equality', but it is an essential prerequisite for women's full participation in political, economic, social and cultural development – from which equality can follow.

To assess relative status among women themselves is more difficult. The status-of-women index shown on this map is meant to be used impressionistically. It elaborates on a method developed by A. Andrews (see Bibliography), whereby countries are ranked on a scale of 0 to 100, relative to the known worst case.

Sources: A. Andrews, 1982; IPPF, 'Women: progress towards equality', 1985; New Internationalist, various issues; UNIESA, Selected Indicators, 1985; UN World Conference for Women, Descriptive List of National Machineries, July 1980.

2 YOUNG BRIDES

Millions of consensual unions lack official blessing by church and state – a fact official statistics fail to take into account. In Latin America the percentage of women in consensual unions ranges from 3 per cent in Chile, and 14 per cent in Peru, to 33 per cent in Guatemala. In Africa most women are in traditional 'marriages' governed only by local custom. In Europe and North America millions of couples 'live together'. In Sweden, for example, among people aged 20–24, 29 per cent are cohabiting while only 22 per cent are married.

National marriage laws seldom apply to everyone, especially in countries where there is great cultural diversity. Legal marriage age minimums alter according to the traditional view of the nature of male-female relations in religious or ethnic groups. Where laws *are* meant to apply universally, the reach of the law may not be long enough to touch groups in physical isolation or those with very strong traditions (as in India – see map).

Legal age minimums for marriage with parental consent range from a low of 12 (for girls) and 14 (for boys) in several Latin American countries, to a high of 22 for women and 20 for men in China. The latter statute is an integral part of China's one-child policy, probably the only country in the world with a higher marital age minimum for women than for men.

Marriage can be big business. In 1983 first-time brides and grooms in the US spent $US 20.1 billion on marriage-related goods and services; *Bride's Magazines* sells 400,000 copies every month. Although dowry has been illegal in India since 1961, a female doctor or civil servant comes with a $US 20–30,000 dowry, and the practice continues to flourish in general. Peasant girls in China fetch $US 150–300 for purchase into marriage, and bride sales are common elsewhere in the world. Arranged marriage also remains common; for example, in Anhui Province, China, it is estimated that 85 per cent are arranged; in South Korea, 40 per cent; in Sri Lanka, 50 per cent.

Marriage can lead to death. Dowry deaths (murder or suicide of a wife for insufficient dowry) are increasing in parts of India; the practice of *sati* (self-immolation or forced suicide by a widow on her husband's funeral pyre) continues.

Sources: Bodrova & R. Anker, 1985; J.E. Brown, 1981; H. Chojnacka, 1980; IPPF, 'Youth in society', 1985; R. Morgan, 1984; K. Newland, 1979; E. Paquot 1982; J.H. Paxman, 1980; PIP, 1980, 'Age at first marriage' 1979; PRB, 'World's women', 1980; J.L. Scherer, 1983; UNIESA, **Marital Status**, 1982; US Department of Commerce, Census, **Women of the World: Sub-Saharan Africa**, 1984; WFS, 1984; WFS and ISI, 1982; **WIN News**, various issues.

3 DOMESTIC DISORDERS

It is hard to find information on domestic violence, which, like rape, is seriously under-reported. The information that is available hints at the magnitude of the problem: in Peru 70 per cent of all crimes reported to the police are of women being beaten by their partners; in one year (1980) in Sao Paulo, Brazil, 772 women were killed by their husbands; in Japan wife-beating has been the second-most frequent reason given for divorce initiated by women. Information on domestic violence other than wife-beating – such as incest – is not available. For wife-rape see Map 37, 'Rape'.

It is only because of the efforts of determined women in a few countries that we know as much as we do about violence in the home. Battered-women's shelters, most of which are filled to capacity all the time, only exist because of women organizing locally. It takes a huge effort to open and sustain women's shelters – often in the face of much opposition and harassment, and usually without support from local or national governments. Statistics on battered-women's shelters given on this map do NOT include various, sometimes numerous, 'hot-lines' and referral centres.

The law lags far behind these efforts. Men's violence against 'their' women and children is accepted (or ignored) across a wide spectrum of cultures. In most countries women have very little legal, or actual, protection from abusive husbands. Feminists are now pushing to have domestic violence recognized as a crime distinct from general assault laws – and for police to have powers of arrest and intervention in cases of domestic assault.

A resurgence in veiling practices is current in many Muslim countries, even where there had previously been no tradition of veiling (for example in Indonesia and Malaysia). Some Muslim women defend the veil, arguing that it is an important cultural identifier, and that it offers a degree of protection from male harassment. There is more general agreement though, that the veil is an enforced abridgement of women's rights, and exists more for men's benefit than women's. Seclusion is a related practice, whereby women are kept confined to their house or family compound. It is regarded as a symbol of a man's wealth and high status.

Domestic violence stems, in part, from the basic fact that women are widely less valued than men, girls less than boys. It is difficult to measure this imbalance. The information on son-preference shown on this map is one of the few sets of data on this topic: it shows 27 countries where parents were asked, as part of the World Fertility Survey, about their preferences for the sex of their children.

Sources: L. Beck & N. Keddie, 1978; Canadian Advisory Council, **Wife-Battering**, 1985; L. Lerman, 1983; Minority Rights Group, **Arab Women**, 1983; R. Morgan, 1984; press reports; B. Warrior, 1985; **WIN News**, Vol. 10, No. 4, 1984; **Women Today**, 22 March 1985.

4 SOCIAL SURGERY

'Social surgery' refers to operations performed for social not medical reasons. (In industrialized nations 'social surgery' includes unnecessary obstetrical, gynecological and plastic surgery – see Map 35, 'Beauty Beat'.)

It is only a decade since African women first dared to speak publicly about female circumcision, but there has been little reduction in its incidence during that time. In Sudan and Somalia, for example, infibulation (the excising of the clitoris, the labia minora and the inner walls of the labia majora, and the suturing of the two sides of the vulva), the most extreme form of circumcision, is practised on nine out of ten girls. Even though it is women who have begun to protest against the practice, it is traditionally women who perform it, and together with men, they encourage its continuation. For as long as women are dependent on marriage for survival, their sexuality will be defined by men, and they will do whatever they must to secure a husband – including mutilation and the preservation of virginity at any cost.

Doctors in Bombay's top hospitals report young upper class Arab and Muslim Indian women paying $US 1500-2000 for 'hymenoplasty', an operation restoring virginity. For all of these women, the question of sexual pleasure is moot.

Female circumcision – especially infibulation – is a major health problem in Africa and the Middle East. Thirty per cent of all Sudanese women have circumcision-related complications. During childbirth infibulated women must be opened surgically; they are sewn up again after birth. Complications can result in the death of the child or the mother. Infant mortality rates are particularly high where the incidence of circumcision is high.

The map shows the documented extent of female circumcision in Africa and the Middle East. It is also practised by Muslims in Malaysia and on the island of Java in Indonesia. According to F. Hosken the map was developed from hospital field reports, the most reliable source of information. As she points out, female circumcision is an ethnic practice and its incidence does not correspond to modern political boundaries. Calculation of the number of women and girls mutilated is based on direct information about the ethnic groups and geographic regions where genital mutilation has been confirmed by local reports. Estimates for Chad, Niger and the Central African Republic in East and Central Africa, and for Benin, Togo, Ghana and Liberia in West Africa are considered very low.

Sources: B. Harden, 'Africans keep rite', 13 July 1985; F. Hosken, 1980, 1982 and May/June 1982; **IPPF News**, various issues; Minority Rights Group, **Female circumcision**, 1983; E.W. Moen, 1983; E. Ogunmodede (n.d.); Population Crisis Committee, **Draper Fund Report**, 1980; D. Russell and N. Van de Ven, 1984; **WIN News**, various issues.

5 SINGLE STATES

The most widely available indicator of 'singleness' is the statistics on the proportion of 'women aged 45–49 never officially married'. These are the women who, in all probability, will never *be* married. Figures do exist on percentages of women who are single, but are not widely collected. The statistics that do exist obscure the fact that women who are in consensual unions (married without benefit of official sanction) are counted – officially – as single. On the other hand, some women do not wish to be identified as single (marriage confers status – see text for Map 2, 'Young Brides'), and so do not reveal their true situation to census takers.

The right to divorce is important for women. Often, however, it means a precipitous drop in an ex-wife's (and usually her children's) standard of living. In the US it is estimated that divorce results in an average decrease of 42 per cent in a woman's income and an *increase* of 73 per cent in a man's.

Divorce rate statistics do not take into account both legal (for example, separation) and illegal (for example, abandonment) marital dissolution other than divorce. Though incomplete, figures do reflect the relative ease or difficulty of obtaining a divorce, including the ability to pay for one, as well as the authority of the prevailing religious system. Catholic countries which have only recently legalized divorce have low rates (for example, Italy). In Muslim countries also divorce is relatively rare; polygyny and social disapproval appear to lower men's need for divorce, while for women it is hardly an option. 'Talaq' – the Muslim practice of simply declaring intent to divorce – is a male prerogative.

In many countries poverty and social stigmatization leave divorced and widowed women in a very precarious social position. (Widows are not even allowed to remarry in some countries.) The 'confirmed bachelor' is a more accepted station than 'spinsterhood'.

Sources: Christian Science Monitor, 24 July 1984; G. Kurian, 1984; PIP, 'Laws and policies', 1984; UN, Demographic Yearbook, 1982; UNIESA, Marital Status, Summary Report, 1982, and Marital Status, Comparative Analysis, 1983; US Department of Commerce, Census, **Women of the World: Near East and North Africa**, 1985, **Asia and the Pacific**, 1985, **Sub-Saharan Africa**, 1984; J. W. Wilkie, 1980; **WIN News**, various issues.

6 MOTHERS

One of the biggest differences between the rich and the poor world lies in the number of children that women have. (This is officially called the 'total fertility rate', and is defined as 'the average number of children that would be born to a woman if she lived through her childbearing years and bore children at the prevailing age-specific rates.') In Western Europe fertility rates are the lowest in the world – and in some cases have dropped below population replacement rates, much to the alarm of many government and military planners. Women in sub-Saharan Africa and the Arab states have the world's highest fertility rates.

The world's 'population problem', therefore, is conventionally defined as a problem of certain countries – and of certain women. But high fertility rates are the consequence of many factors. It is closely related to age at marriage; where early marriage for girls is encouraged (see Map 2, 'Young Brides'), women will spend a longer part of their lives in childbearing, and will have more children. As it stands, the interval between the first and last birth for women in Kenya is almost 19 years; in Jordan, 18 years; in Syria and Mexico, 17 years – compared with 7 years in the United States. Fertility is linked to knowledge of and access to contraceptives – which is usually a function of state policy (see Map 7, 'Population Policies' and Notes). Many population programmes are designed only to persuade women to use contraceptives, not to educate them about contraception – resulting in a high failure rate. High fertility is linked to poverty and its related high infant mortality rates: to end up with a family of four or five, a woman may bear ten children. In poorer and agricultural economies children are an economic asset. In many countries a woman's status goes with the number of children she bears. More to the point, in many countries men feel that their 'manhood' is proved by the number of children they can father.

Infertility is less well documented, but affects a significant proportion of women around the world; the average infertility rate in sub-Saharan Africa is 12 per cent. Since women's status is often determined by their ability to bear children, infertility can be a particular hardship – and often a serious threat to health. Where a couple cannot have children, the problem is almost invariably put down to the woman's infertility.

New reproductive technologies are being developed, ostensibly to help women with reproductive difficulties. In fact, the benefits are available to only a few, and the structure of these new reproductive technologies is such that women's control over the reproductive process is jeopardized; women become the providers of the raw materials (eggs, ovaries) for an industrial process of reproduction that is largely controlled by the male doctors and technicians developing the technologies.

Sources: Council of Europe, Family Formation, 1982; K.T. de Graft-Johnson, 1980; G. Kurian, 1984; PRB, '1984 World population data sheet'; UN, Demographic Yearbook, 1981, 1983, 1984; UN Decade for Women, Selected Statistics, 1985; UN Fund for Population Activities Compendium (yearly); UNIESA, The World Population Situation in 1983, 1984; US Department of Commerce, Women of the World: Sub-Saharan Africa, 1984; Women's Emergency Conference, 1985; World Bank, World Development Report, 1984.

7 POPULATION POLICIES

The population policies of most governments are difficult to interpret. Only a few governments have clearly defined and explicit policies. The one-child policy of China is well known, and is one of the most explicit population policies in the world. Romania currently has one of the most repressive – and also explicit – policies, limiting women's access to contraceptives and family planning services (see Notes to Map 9, 'Abortion').

Pro-natalist governments want women to have more children, usually to bolster military strength. Some governments, such as France, East Germany and Finland have official pro-natalism stances, but they do not enforce it. Other governments, such as Kuwait, Chad and Laos go to great lengths to bolster pro-natalism – by outlawing contraceptives, clamping down on abortions, and offering hefty incentives to women to have large numbers of children. At its worst, pro-natalism can effectively mean forced breeding for women.

The majority of the world's governments have policies designed to reduce or stabilize the population, and most support family planning to some extent. 'Strong' government support for family planning usually means that the government sponsors educational programmes, supports clinics, distributes contraceptives and offers incentives to women to have fewer children. In 'direct support' countries, governments may subsidize family planning clinics or encourage educational programmes, but involvement ranges from being systematic to being quite casual. 'Indirect support' usually means simply that the government allows private family planning agencies to operate – or otherwise does not erect legislative barriers.

Like pro-natalism, population *reduction* policies can slip over into coercion. Sterilization abuse (which includes forced sterilization and sterilization without informed consent) is widespread, though can only be documented for a handful of countries. Other forms of reproductive abuses – for example the charges of forced abortions in China – are almost impossible to document. We make no attempt to map them here, but *do* note that they exist.

National government population policy is often influenced by and dependent upon international aid. With the exception of India and China (which mainly finance their own population programmes), foreign aid pays for an average of 50 per cent of all population programmes in poorer countries. International population aid is generally beneficial to women – and, in fact, more of it is needed since millions of women in the world have no access to family planning services. But dependency on foreign aid leaves women vulnerable to policies and decisions made well beyond their country and beyond their reach. Family planning aid becomes a political tool – it may be withdrawn, increased or decreased for reasons that have nothing to do with women's health or their reproductive choices. This is most clearly illustrated by the current shift in US government policies that are jeopardizing the ability of women the world over to make reproductive choices. The US government is imposing an anti-abortion morality on all funding decisions, and has withdrawn support from major population agencies (including the International Federation for Planned Parenthood and the UN Fund for Population Activities) because these agencies do not condemn abortion. Family planning for millions of women hangs in the balance.

Sources: Boston Women's Health Book Collective (file materials); Family Planning in the 1980s; PIP, 'Laws and policies' 1984; PRB, 'Family planning', 1981; UN, World Population Trends, 1981 and 1983; UN Fund for Population Activities; UNIESA The World Population Situation, 1984; World Bank, World Development Report 1984.

8 CONTRACEPTION

Women the world over face the dilemma that 'effective contraceptives tend to be unsafe, and safe contraceptives tend not to be effective'. For many women contraceptives are not available at all. Making contraceptives and making them available to women rests in the hands of governments, pharmaceutical manufacturers, and international aid agencies – all of which may be working at odds with one another, and with the women for whom the contraceptives are intended. Women's voices and women's needs often get lost in the labyrinth of big business, big bureaucracy, and international policy-making.

Virtually all contraceptives manufacturers are subsidiaries of large multinational pharmaceutical firms. The world market is dominated by five companies: Wyeth Labs (USA), Ortho Pharmaceuticals (USA), G.D. Searle (USA), Syntex (USA), and Schering AG (West Germany). The most profitable contraceptive is 'the Pill', an estimated 54 million women worldwide are on it. But new products are constantly being tested – often by the dubious means of trying it out on women in poor countries before marketing it in industrial nations. The current controversy over the new injectable contraceptive, 'DepoProvera', is due in part to this sort of testing programme. Lawsuits and public outcry over the DepoProvera case and the faulty and dangerous IUD, the 'Dalkon Shield', have prompted the major manufacturers to retreat from product development and testing. There are few developments in male contraceptives since neither private nor public research money is directed toward it.

In Third World countries most contraceptives are distributed through the public sector. Governments and family planning agencies buy contraceptives from the pharmaceutical companies and distribute them free or at cost. The major world suppliers of contraceptive aid are: Agency for International Development (AID), the UN Fund for Population Activities, Swedish International Development Authority (SIDA), and International Planned Parenthood Federation (IPPF). Millions of women are dependent on these four for contraceptives supply – which also means that these women are vulnerable to policy changes made thousands of miles away, shifts in funding priorities, or shifting political favours.

Sources: Drug Store News, various issues; D.L. Nortman, 1982; E. Paquot, 1982; PIP, 'Oral contraceptives', 1982; PRB, 'Fertility and status', 1981; UN, **World Population Trends**, 1981 and 1983; S. Urang, 1983; US Congress, Office of Technology Assessment Technologies, 1982; World Bank, **World Development Report**, 1984; World Pharmaceutical News, Scrip, 1981–84.

9 ABORTION

Thirty to fifty-five million abortions occur annually, about half of which are illegal, and half of which take place in poor countries.

Most abortions are undergone by married, older women with completed families. In the West and in urban Africa it is mostly younger, unmarried women who have abortions in order to postpone childbearing. The main reasons for women choosing abortion are lack of or failure of contraception, a change in personal circumstances (for example, desertion, widowhood, financial problems), or detection of birth defects. (In India amniocentesis – originally developed to detect fetal abnormalities – is increasingly being used to establish fetal gender, followed by abortion of females.)

In poor countries illegal abortion kills 50–1000 women per 100,000 procedures. It is 10–250 times more dangerous to have an abortion there as it is to use any form of birth control. Up to 70 per cent of maternal deaths are due to complications following illegal abortion. Legalization of abortion reduces maternal mortality, especially where abortions are also affordable and widely available (legalization does not guarantee access).

Some religions tolerate abortion, some do not. Where church and state are intertwined, abortion laws follow religious dictates, as in Muslim and some Catholic countries. Government population policy can also determine abortion law: on International Women's Day in 1984, Romanian President Ceausescu declared that 'it is every healthy Romanian woman's duty to have four children'. In an attempt to increase the labour force, stringent anti-abortion laws were suddenly brought in. Monthly gynaecological checks for women in the state's industrial complexes were instituted to insure that no woman had a (now-illegal) abortion. On the other hand, the perceived need to reduce population in Singapore and Tunisia resulted in liberalized laws. In Cyprus abortion following rape was legalized after that country's civil war; war-time rape of women by soldiers necessitated the change. Doctors and midwives making a good living off illegal abortion effectively oppose abortion and contraception availability in some countries in the Middle East and South East Asia.

Reliable data on abortion is hard to come by. Reported, legal abortions are often a fraction of the true abortion rate; and there is no reliable data on the incidence of illegal abortion – only best guesses.

Sources: R. Cook, et al., 1977; George Washington University, 'Pregnancy termination', 1973 and 'Law and policy', 1976; International Reference Center, **Abortion Research Notes**, 1983, 1984; G. Kurian, 1984; E.G. Moore-Cavar, 1974;
R. Morgan, 1984; Population Council, 1984; Populatin Crisis Committee, '**Improving the Status of women**, 1980 and **Population**, 1982; Population Institute, 1984; F. Sanchez-Torres, 1980; C. Tietze, 1983; UN, Demographic Yearbook, 1981, 1982; P. Wise, 1984; A. Wolfson, 1983.

One-quarter of all deaths in the world occur among children under five, two-thirds of whom are infants. Ninety-seven per cent of infant deaths happen in developing countries. Three million infants die each year in India alone; another two million in Bangladesh, Nigeria, Indonesia and Pakistan combined.

Infant mortality rates could be dramatically lowered through primary health care (see Notes to Map 26, 'Illness and Health') providing midwifery, encouragement to breastfeed, vaccinations, QRT (oral-rehydration therapy against diarrhoea), and antibiotics against infection.

Changes in women's social condition would also make a difference. Girls and women in school delay childbearing. This results in both lowered infant (and maternal) mortality rates and educated mothers with greater opportunities in life. High infant mortality itself encourages high birth rates – to replace children who have died. When infant mortality rates drop, fewer and healthier children are born.

The infant mortality rate statistics used here represent five-year averages to avoid using occasionally skewed single-year figures. The USSR rate is considered very conservative; it is known to be rising as a result of annual flu epidemics, increasing alcoholism, poor prenatal care, high abortion rates and declining breastfeeding. Official statistics have been unavailable since 1974.

Abortion is a leading cause of maternal mortality in some countries. Where abortion is legal abortion rates do not necessarily decline, but maternal deaths from abortion do. In Latin America abortion accounts for 30–50 per cent of all maternal deaths; it is the leading cause in Caracas, according to estimates. In India one woman dies from a septic abortion every ten minutes.

Maternal mortality is an important index of a community's commitment to women's health care. Maternal-related deaths are among the leading causes of death for women aged 15–44 in poor countries. It is the leading or second-leading cause of death in one-third of these countries. Adequate prenatal and birth care could prevent most of those deaths resulting from toxaemia, haemorrhage, sepsis, anaemia, obstructed labour and other complications. Teenage women having too many babies too quickly, who are inadequately nourished and rested, face an unacceptable high risk of death in childbirth.

Maternal mortality statistics are often not collected, or if collected are not reported (for example in the USSR, mentioned above), especially where rates are known to be high. Where rates *are* reported, they are often under-reported. In countries with well-developed health care systems and well-documented statistics, rates average 5–30 deaths per 100,000 live births. In parts of Africa rates of 1000 per 100,000 live births have been reported. Everywhere rates are higher for poor and minority women.

Sources: W.U. Chandler, 1984; M. Feshbach, 1982; Pakistan, Ministry of Information and Broadcasting, **Women in Pakistan** (n.d.); P. Huston, 1978; M. Islam, 1977; R. Morgan, 1984; K. Newland, 1981; PAHO, 1982; C. Tietze, 1977; UN, **Demographic Yearbook**, 1982; UN World Conference for Women, **Statistical Abstract**, 1980; UNICEF, **State of World's Children, 1984** and **1985**, and **Assignment Children**, 1980; US Department of Commerce, Census, **Women in the World: Latin American and the Caribbean**, 1984; WHO, **Sixth Report**, 1980; Women for Women, 1977; World Bank, **Development Report 1984**.

11 BIRTH CARE

'Midwife' is an umbrella term that actually includes two different types of birth attendants: a) 'traditional birth attendants', usually rural women, midwives by practice and by tradition, but without medical training; b) 'midwife', usually women with some medical training, and often with some sort of accreditation.

The percentage of births attended by trained personnel (doctors, nurses, trained midwives) varies considerably according to region. In Africa only 34 per cent of all births are attended by a medically-trained attendant; in Asia the figure is 49 per cent; in Latin America, 64 per cent; in Europe, 97 per cent; and in North America, 100 per cent. These figures reflect the role of traditional birth attendants in providing maternity support to the world's women. The World Health Organization estimates that 45 per cent of all babies in the world are delivered by traditional birth attendants. Midwives and traditional birth attendants (the overwhelming majority of whom are women) together deliver about 80 per cent of all babies in the Third World.

The aim of most governments is to turn their traditional birth attendants into midwives. To this end, traditional birth attendants have been outlawed in a number of countries, including Egypt, Lebanon, and the Sudan. Until recently, midwives were outlawed in North America. Over the past century the powerful medical establishment there went to great lengths to eradicate midwives; doctors saw midwives as competition and as a threat to their monopoly on medical knowledge. Midwifery survived, though, and is now enjoying a comeback in most industrial countries.

Sources: Council of Europe, 1975; D.L. Nortman, 1982; M. Owen, 1983; PIP, 'Traditional midwives and family planning', 1980; **Statistical Yearbook for Asia and the Pacific**, 1982; UN Decade for Women, **Selected Statistics**, 1985; UNICEF, **State of World's Children 1985**; WHO, **Coverage of Maternity Care**, 1985, **Health and Status of Women**, 1980, and **World Health Statistics**, 1983.

12 FAMILIES

Conventional definitions of 'family' revolve around the presence of children. Because women everywhere have primary responsibility for childcare, 'the family' for them is as much a work unit as an emotional one. But the workload on women varies widely. This is suggested by the dependency ratio presented on the main map: the ratio of pre-school children (under age five) to women. Higher dependency ratios mean that direct childcare demands (feeding, health care, etc.) are greater, and indirect demands, such as agricultural labour, and water and firewood collecting are also greater.

The demands of childcare are what keep women most confined to the home, and keep them out of the waged workforce. Out-of-the-home childcare is radically short of the need for it, worldwide. Only the Scandinavian and Eastern European governments recognize childcare as a legitimate public policy responsibility. Elsewhere women must either patch together whatever help they can find (usually relying on older family members) or pay a large share of their income on private childcare (a growing problem now in the USA). As more and more women form single-parent households (see Map 28, 'Poverty') through divorce or choice, the childcare crisis will grow.

Global trends indicate that the nuclear family is slowly replacing the extended family as the standard household configuration. Consequently household sizes are shrinking. The smallest households are found in Europe; the largest in the Arab states. Twelve countries report an average household size of over six people: Afghanistan, Algeria, Bahrain, Botswana, Fiji, Kenya, Kiribati, Kuwait, Maldives, Nicaragua, Surinam, and Syria.

With the notable exception of North America it is unusual – and often unacceptable – for anyone, but especially women, to live alone – women's lives in most places are lived entirely in the context of a family. Although it is women's role as mothers that appears to give 'families' their raison d'etre, control of the family usually runs through the men involved. Women live in the house and in the family of their father/husband/brother. In this way the family forms the primary unit of social control, particularly over women. It is for this reason that many feminists argue that social change for women must start with the family – and the conclusion that 'the personal is political' derives largely from this sort of analysis.

Sources: V. Bodrova, & R. Anker, 1985; G. Kurian, 1984; C. Lemke, 1985; **New Internationalist**, Dec 1982; PRB, 'Changing American family', 1983; Statistics Sweden, 1985; UN Decade for Women, **Selected Statistics**, 1985; UN, **Demographic Yearbook**, 1981 and 1982; UNECA, **Demographic Data Sheets**, 1983, and **Day Care**,1981; UN World Conference for Women, **Statistical Abstract**, 1980.

13 TIME BUDGETS

The unequal division of labour is universal. Our most deeply ingrained assumptions about a woman's proper place – in the home and taking care of children – determine the way women spend their time. In poor and rich countries alike it is women – with a few exceptions – who do the subsistence work: feeding, clothing, tending and tilling – in short, managing their families' survival. And very few women see themselves as 'just housewives'; in Tamil Nadu, India, for example, poor women see their role as 'earning for and supporting the family'.

All over the globe there is still 'women's work' and 'men's work'; but the traditional divisions of labour by sex are breaking down – on women's side. In rich countries, where women are increasingly part of the workforce, they do a double shift: in the office or factory by day and then at domestic chores by night. In Italy, 85 per cent of husbands do no housework; in the UK 72 per cent of housework is done 'mostly by women'. In the US more than half of the female labour force is married and the biggest increase in employment has been among women with pre-school children. This results not only in overwork but also in handicapped job prospects: a young mother cannot work overtime, travel or be flexible enough for company promotions.

In poor countries traditional family structures are breaking down as men are drawn to the cities and into the cash economy. Yet for women 'economic development' often means more work and less control of resources. Husbands are less likely to help out as they are freed from traditional male domestic responsibilities – but women are expected to assist in their husband's cash crop production in addition to maintaining their own family plots. Training for double-duty begins early, as children imitate their parents. In Zaire, for example, girls do 55 per cent as much work around the house as their mothers, boys only 15 per cent.

The value of women's unpaid labour is estimated at 25–40 per cent of measured GNP in industrialized countries. Another estimate values it as adding one-third – or $US 4000 billion – to the world's economic product.

'Equal opportunity' and 'economic development' must not merely translate into an opportunity for women to work more and control less. The greatest injustice is perhaps to be found as much in inequality in the home as in the workplace.

Information for this spread mostly comes from individual researchers' field data, sometimes published by the international development agencies or the UN. Governments in the West are just beginning to sponsor collection of time-use data; until recently what went on behind closed doors held no interest for official statisticians.

Sources: M. Acharya et al., 1979; Austrian Federal Ministry of Social Affairs (n.d.); L. Beneria, 1984; V. Bodrova & R. Anker, 1985; J.E. Brown, 1981; B.M. Buvinic et al., 1978; CEC, European Women and Men, 1978; Consumers Association of Penang, 1982; R. Dixon, 1978; FAO, 1983; L. Goldschmidt-Clermont, 1983; ILO, Womanpower, 1975; ISIS, 'Motherhood', 1982; G. Lapidus, 1978; New Internationalist, July 1985; K. Newland, 1980; OECD, 1975; D. Ramprakash, 1986; A.K.N. Reddy, 1980; B. Rogers, 1980; R. L. Sivard, 1985; Social and Cultural Planning, Netherlands, 1985; Statistics Sweden, 1985; UNECA, Critical Needs, 1981. Integration of Women, 1974, and Women of Africa, 1975; UNICEF, Assignment Children, 1980, and Situation of Women in Kenya, 1985; World Bank, World Development Report 1984.

14 AGRICULTURE

Women produce most of the food for home comsumption and are an important part of the paid agricultural labour force. They harvest coffee in Rwanda, pick bananas and pineapples in Martinique and tea in Sri Lanka and farm shrimp in coastal India. They are also active as traders and marketers. In Ghana, over 87 per cent of traders are women. Women also keep small animals for sale at market and use at home. Women's agricultural labour is not normally given much consideration in agricultural development schemes or in education, training, financial credit and extension programmes. Yet it is women who make many of the most critical agricultural decisions, from which seed to plant to when and how to harvest.

In Africa, only five per cent of all trained agricultural personnel are female. In 13 African countries they make up less than one per cent, and in only four countries are they over ten per cent. Women represent approximately half of all agricultural students in the USSR and Romania; in the UK and Australia, around 15 per cent and in Ecuador and Swaziland, fewer than five per cent. In Africa, technical and credit assistance for women, such as it is, is concentrated in home economics (where 100 per cent of students are female).

Modernization of agriculture often means mechanization of production and land 'reform'. The new (high) technology lightens men's workloads because it is used to help produce cash crops and shift male work patterns away from home. Women's work increases because of the loss of male help in subsistence farming and the loss of control over any crops which may have started to procure money. Land 'reform' often means a shift from traditional (often communal or even matrilineal) to private and/or patrilineal land ownership, denying women access to land they have long farmed for their families and to any cash it might generate.

In the USA the role of farmers' wives in farm management and agricultural production is often overlooked. Women in the USA only *own* five per cent of all farms, though this is a two-fold increase over the past decade.

Sources: G. Ashworth, 'Daughters', (n.d); K. Cloud, 1977; C. D. Deere and M. Léon de Leal, 1982; Demography (monthly); FAO, Information Note, 1983; E. Hong, 1983; ILO, Yearbook 1982; ISIS, 'Women, land and food', 1979; M. McAndrew and J. Peers, (n.d.); R. Morgan, 1984; New York Times, 15 October 1984; PRB, World's Women Data Sheet 1980; Rogers, 1979; Safilios-Rothschild, Conventional Indicators, 1983; UN Decade for Women, (K) Rural Development, 1984 and Selected Statistics, 1985; UNESCAP, 'Reflections of decade'; UNESCO, Yearbook, 1982; UN World Conference for Women, Women in Rural Areas, 1980; US Department of Commerce, Census, Women of the World: Asia and the Pacific, 1985, Near East and North Africa, 1985, Latin America and the Caribbean, 1984, and Sub-Saharan Africa, 1984; World Bank, World Development Report 1984.

15 LABOUR FORCE

Official statistics on women in the labour force are the only broad-based economic indicators according to sex available internationally. But there are serious flaws in the definitions of 'work', 'labour force', and 'economic activity' – flaws that tend to mean that much of women's work is overlooked. Further, the quality of data and the definitions used vary from country to country. So, while the general impression of labour force activity worldwide is fairly reliably portrayed, the figures are not sufficiently accurate to support elaborate interpretations. Since the International Labour Organization (ILO) is virtually the only agency that collects and compiles international labour force data, it is not possible to confirm, compare, or criticise their figures using alternative sources. The ILO has consistently made an effort to collect and report data by sex – and they have done better at this than almost any other of the large international agencies.

Labour force statistics generally include only formally structured waged work – work, for example, for which there is official employee registration. Much of women's work falls beyond these boundaries. Millions of women work in the informal sector (as domestic servants or market traders, for example) and this labour goes uncounted. At the far end of the work continuum is all of the unpaid labour done by women; Maps 13, 'Time Budgets', and 14, 'Agriculture', deal with this phenomenon and help to provide a more balanced view of the world's work done by women.

The reported decrease over time in African women's labour force participation is most likely due to methods of counting and compiling labour statistics. The decrease in the USSR is more likely explained by shifts in the demographic balance between women and men since the end of World War Two.

Sources: A. Cropper, 1980; ILO, Women at Work, various issues, World Labour Report, 1985, and Yearbook, 1984; R. Morgan, 1984; R. L. Sivard, 1985; UN Decade for Women, (A) Employment, 1984, and Selected Statistics, 1985; WIN News, Spring 1984.

16 OUT TO WORK

One of the biggest worldwide economic shifts this century is the entry of women into the paid labour market. Some women have always worked for wages; the big change is that now women of all classes and ages work. However, it is still much more true for women than men that participation in the labour force is influenced by such factors as marital status, age and family responsibilities. Marriage and childbearing are the two most important influences that keep women out of the waged workforce. In a number of countries (amoung them, Lichtenstein, Rwanda, Burundi, Swaziland, and the Philippines) husbands have the legal right to restrict their wives' choice to work outside the home and, in some cases, to prohibit it altogether. Many employers discriminate against hiring married women, whether or not this is within the law.

Women's wages are vital to their own survival and that of their families. This is clearly the case in single-parent families. A 1984 study in the UK showed that homes with married women working are 35 per cent better off than homes without. Other studies show that women spend a greater proportion of their income than men on family necessities such as food and shelter.

While more and more women go out to work, most social structures and government policies are constructed as though the stay-at-home wife was the norm. The lack of childcare facilities (see Map 12, 'Families') is the most striking indication of this conflict.

The cautions about data in the notes for Map 15, 'Labour Force', generally apply to the data on this map too.

Sources: CEC, Supplement 15, 1984; ILO, Women at Work, No. 2, 1982, World Labour Report, 1985, and Yearbook, 1982, 1983 and 1984; M. Mukhopadhyay, 1984; R.L. Sivard, 1985; UN Decade for Women, (A) Employment, 1984; US Department of Labor, Handbook, 1983; WIN News, various issues; Women of Europe, Jan 1985.

17 MIGRANT WORKERS

Migration is usually treated as though it were a predominantly male experience. In fact, women are an important and growing proportion of the world's migrants, and some migrant streams consist almost entirely of women. A 1985 study by the US Department of Labor showed that 66 per cent of all immigrants to the United States are now women – a rise from 41 per cent at the turn of the century.

The patterns of women's migration, and of work in the host country, are distinctive. Women who move to cities from rural areas typically face severe discrimination, and end up being employed in the worst paid and least regulated work sectors. Domestic service and the garment industry are, universally, job ghettos for migrant women. Prostitution is often taken up as a last resort. Women's migration is closely linked to the growing feminization of poverty, the increasing feminization of agriculture, and increasing prostitute exploitation (see related Maps 28, 'Poverty', and 36, 'Sex for Sale').

The line between voluntary and forced migrations is sometimes very thin. Migrants who are fleeing harsh economic conditions are often no better off than refugees. Governments occasionally encourage migration as part of a planned economic programme: overseas workers can be a major source of foreign currency, and migration can alleviate labour problems at home. Women's lives are affected by migration even when they themselves do not move. Male migration is an important factor in increasing rural female poverty and in the increase in women-headed households.

Some migration patterns change rapidly, and international reporting cannot keep pace. Statistics on migrants, therefore, should be used with caution, and may indicate migrant streams that are no longer current.

Sources: The Economist, 3 December 1983; ILO, World Labour Report, 1985; Inside Asia, Nov/Dec 1984; ISIS 'Migrant women', 1980; Migration Today, No.s 30 & 31, 1983, No. 33, 1984; Minority Rights Group, Western Europe's Migrant Workers, 1982; A. Phizacklea, 1983; Population Crisis Committee, 'World population growth', 1983; UN Decade for Women, (A) Employment, 1984; USAID, Women in International Migration, 1980.

18 JOB GHETTOS

The map depicting job ghettos around the world does NOT show 'the jobs where most women work'; it shows the jobs where most of the workers are women – it shows the jobs that are typically feminized. We are not suggesting, for example, that most women who work in the UK work at office cleaning, but we are saying that most office cleaners are women.

There is a marked worldwide division into 'women's' and 'men's' jobs, but the set of women's jobs is not the same in every country. 'Women's work' in Sri Lanka is tea picking; in Nigeria it is market trading; in the USA it is nursing, childcare, primary school teaching, for example. 'Women's work' is usually considered undignified for men to do, and in any event it is usually too poorly paid and menial to attract competition from male workers. Men's jobs, on the other hand, are often well-paid and highly respected, and women have a very hard time breaking into their ranks.

The increasingly internationalized industrial production system in textiles and electronics has created a widespread common job ghetto: women electronics workers in the USA and in Singapore,often work for the same employer. The creation of these female job ghettos is often an integral part of government economic planning. Many governments in South East Asia, for example, actively try to attract foreign investment by promising a docile, willing, hard working labour pool of young women.

Sources: V. Bodrova & R. Anker, 1985; W. Chapkis & C. Enloe, 1983; A. Fuentes & B. Ehrenreich, 1983; M. Gill & J. Massiah, 1984; ILO, **Problems of women non-manual workers**, 1981, and **Yearbook**, 1984; R. Morgan, 1984; S. Quinn-Judge, 1983; UNECA, **Mozambique**, 1980; UNESCAP, **Social Development Newsletter**, No. 10, 1984; US Department of Labor, **Time of Change**, 1984; **WIN News**, various issues.

19 EARNINGS

Women's experience of the workplace is different from men's. The earnings gap is among those differences – and derives from a set of interconnections that describe many women's working conditions. Women's low wages result in part from their ghettoization in certain jobs, the fact that most part-time work is done by women, and the lack of job training provided by menial and part-time work. In turn, low wages prevent women from 'getting ahead' and escaping their restrictive job choices.

An increasing proportion of all people who are 'poor' are the wage-earning poor: people who work, but whose wages fall below minimum needs. Women are a large proportion of this new class. Since pensions and other benefits are usually based on earnings, women's low earning at work has ripple effects throughout their lives.

Figures on wage comparison represent the total wage *earnings* of women and men – that is, what the average woman and man bring home as a pay packet at the end of a day, week or year. They do not necessarily represent wage per hour (or wage per week) comparisons.

The job categories used for specific wage comparisons include a wide range. 'Professional and technical workers' include librarians, lawyers, doctors, nurses, writers, engineers, teachers. 'Managers and administrators' include sales managers and all administrators in both private and public sector jobs. 'Craft workers' mostly consist of bakers, brick masons, carpenters, machinists, and electricians.

Part-time work is a mixed blessing for women: it offers a way for them to combine waged work with domestic responsibilities, but it leaves them economically marginalized. Women who work part-time are more ghettoized into low-esteem, low-paying jobs than women working full-time. Part-time workers usually receive no benefits, pension coverage or union protection. Because women are encouraged to work part-time – to be exploited workers *and* 'superwomen' – men are allowed to continue avoiding family and household responsibilities. The fact that part-time work is mainly a female phenomenon reflects, in part, the attitudes of men to family responsibilities. Of all part-time workers in the UK, 94 per cent are women; in West Germany, also 94 per cent; in Sweden, 85 per cent; in Australia, 79 per cent; in the USA, 70 per cent. In 1984 the Iranian government legislated that women who work in offices or factories can work *only* half-time – on the basis that women's work is not very valuable in the first place, and that women should properly be devoting most of their time to being wives and mothers.

Sources: CEC, **Supplement 10**, 1982; Eurostat, 1980; ILO, **Chart**, 1984, **Problems of Women Non-Manual Workers**, 1981, and **Women at Work**, various issues; A. McAuley, 1981; R. Morgan, 1984; press reports; N. Rytina, 1982; R.L. Sivard, 1985; UNESCO, **Yearbook**, 1981; UN Decade for Women, **(A) Employment**, 1984; **WIN News**, various issues.

20 JOB PROTECTION

Women are more likely than men to become unemployed, especially when jobs are scarce – so, 'hard times' often hit women hardest of all. 'Youth unemployment' is usually portrayed as mostly a male problem, but in fact it is as much, or more, of a problem for women:

Unemployment rates for people under age 25, 1981, USA   percentages

	Men	Women
Whites	13.7	11.7
Blacks	30.6	31.7
Hispanics	17.0	17.8

The prevailing attitude that work is less serious and less important for women than for men, often means that women's unemployment is treated as a trivial concern. But with more and more families worldwide relying wholly or partly on women's wages, unemployment is a major problem – and , in turn, fuels the growing feminization of poverty (see Map 28, 'Poverty').

As a general rule, official records of unemployment undercount the unemployed – and never take into account the 'underemployed' (people who are working a part-time or poorly paid job simply because no appropriate job exists): this means that women's actual unemployment could be as much as two-times higher than reported.

Maternity often brings unemployment for women. There are *very* few safeguards to protect women's right to a job – and to maternity leave – during and after pregnancy. In many countries the maternity leave policies on the books remain unenforced and have little effect on private employers who routinely fire or 'ease out' pregnant workers. The USA stands worst among industrial nations in providing maternity protection – the only protection that women in the USA have is whatever they can work out privately with their employer. Maternity leave has yet to be taken seriously as a public policy issue.

Women at work tend to be much less unionized than men – in part because many women work in socially-isolated, hard-to-organize jobs: domestic service, or home-work piece-assembly, for example. Sometimes men, fearing competition, act to block women's entry to unionized labour. The end result is that women's rate of particip-ation in unions lags far behind their participation in the labour market. Furthermore, with the exception of Eastern European countries, women have little voice in union power structures.

Sources: CEC, Supplement No. 9, 1982, and Supplement No. 10, 1982; European Documentation, 1984; ILO, Women at Work, No. 2, 1982, and No. 2, 1984, World Labor Report, 1985 and Yearbook, 1984; R. Morgan, 1984; R.L. Sivard, 1985; UN World Conference for Women, Report, 1980; US Department of Labor, Time of Change, 1984.

21 ACCESS TO MEANS

It is difficult to make cross-cultural comparisons of women's land rights. There is no international survey of these rights, and there is often little uniformity within a single country; women's land rights may vary according to local tribal, religious, or customary laws. On related topics, such as women's access to credit, there is no international data at all.

The status of women with regard to property is closely related to the concept 'head of household' – the head of household is generally accorded authority over joint property. If men are automatically assumed to be the household head, then in the normal state of affairs it is assumed that men will control all property, even property jointly acquired.

In most countries men still have the right to determine choice of married domicile. For most women this means that when they get married they leave their home and family to join the household of their husband. In doing this they forfeit any property rights they may have held in their name. For many women in the world, becoming married also means becoming landless. In countries where women have an equal right to choose the married domicile, this is a very recent change: almost nowhere did women have this right before the 1970s. In Switzerland women only won this right in 1983. The idea that women should be entitled to a share of their husband's wealth acquired during marriage is an even more recent and more radical legal departure – and in most countries women do not have this protection.

In general women worldwide have access to wealth and resources primarily through their husbands or fathers – they do not have independent means. Inter-national aid is also generally directed to, and by, men. Two international organiz-ations are working to change this: Women's World Banking is an international banking organization offering loans to Third World women; the UN Voluntary Fund for Women raises money for development projects for women.

Sources: FAO, 1979; C. Heckathorn, 1980; R. Hirschon, 1984; A.E. Mayer; R. Morgan, 1984; B. Rogers, 1979; UN Decade for Women, World Survey on the Role of Women in Development, 1984; WIN News, Summer 1984; Women of Europe, various issues.

22 SCHOOL DAYS

Girls' access to basic education has improved greatly over the past two decades. There was an 'enrolment boom' in the 1960s and 1970s that pushed girls into the classroom as never before. But inequities still exist: boys are more educated than girls, and girls in rich countries and in cities are more educated than those in poor countries or rural settings.

In Burkina Faso, Ethiopia, Bhutan, Afghanistan and Papua New Guinea, among others, fewer than 10 per cent of primary age girls were in school in 1960. In 1980 percentages ranged from a virtually unchanged 11 per cent in Afghanistan to an impressive 54 per cent in Papua New Guinea. By contrast, in countries as diverse as Guyana, Portugal, the USSR, Kuwait and New Zealand, virtually all eligible girls attended primary school then as they do now. In cities all over the globe, more girls go to school than do their rural counterparts; in Burundi, 60 per cent of eligible urban girls attend school compared with 7 per cent of rural girls; in Guatemala the ratio is 66 per cent to 30 per cent; in Nepal it is 36 per cent to 4 per cent. These differences are most acute in countries where enrolments are low overall.

Educational 'ghettos' exist for girls and for boys, but boys have more and better choices than do girls. In vocational secondary schools in France in 1980, for every 100 boys, there were 5 girls in horticulture, 58 in arts and crafts and 14,000 in secretarial schools. Less than one girl per 100 boys registered for electrical or engineering trades training.

Data is based on 'enrolment *ratios*' – the proportion of eligible children attending schools – not rates (the actual number of children attending).

Sources: E. Bartunek, C. Bohm & I. Gross, 1984; V. Bodrova and R. Anker, 1985; CEC, **Supplement No.s 10 and 11**, 1982 and **14**, 1984; D. Davin, 1976; European Documentation, 1984; E.W. Fernea, 1985; M. McAndrew & J. Peers (n.d.); Pakistan, Ministry of Information and Broadcasting, **Women in Pakistan** (n.d.); E. Hong, 1983; IPPF, 'Youth' wallchart, 1985; UNESCO, **Women and Development**, 1981; UNICEF, **State of World's Children 1985**; US Department of Commerce, Census, **Illustrative Statistics**, 1980, and **Women of the World: Asia and Pacific**, 1985, **Latin America and Caribbean**, 1984, **Near East and North Africa**, 1985, **Sub-Saharan Africa**, 1984; World Bank, **World Tables**, 1984.

23 HIGHER EDUCATION

Women began entering university in the mid- to late-19th century in the USA, Canada, and the UK. Elsewhere in the world universities opened up in the post-World War Two period. Dramatic enrolment increases occurred, averaging 30 per cent of the total for poor countries worldwide. Between 1965 and 1985 estimated enrolment in Qatar and South Yemen increased from nought to 57 per cent and 19 per cent of the total respectively; in Guatemala from 9 per cent to 28 per cent; and in Brazil from 25 per cent to 48 per cent.

Today the world picture looks like this:

Women's share of higher education, 1985 UN estimates

North America	49	Europe	45
Asia and USSR	33	Africa	29
Australia and New Zealand	46	Latin America and Caribbean	45

The percentage of women faculty instructors has not increased nearly as dramatically as have student enrolments. In the USA in 1870 women represented 12 per cent of the teaching staff in universities; in 1880, 36 per cent; and in 1890, dropped to 20 per cent, averaging about one-quarter from then until today. The proportion has not increased since 1910.

In 1870 in the US, 21 per cent of all university students were women. Since then enrolment rates have fluctuated, peaking around 1930 and again in the 1940s. In 1944 50 per cent of BAs and MAs were awarded to women. A sharp postwar decline followed when war veterans flooded the schools. Women were encouraged to stay at home instead of competing with 'needier' men for school slots and jobs.

The terms university, college, post-secondary, third-level and higher education are used almost interchangeably in the literature; but the last two are the most inclusive.

Sources: G. Ashworth, 'Daughters' (n.d); O. Carmichael, 1959; CEC, **Supplement Nos. 10 & 14**; Collier's Encyclopedia, 1985; Encyclopedia Britannica, 1985; E.W. Fernea, 1985; S. Harris, 1972; International Association of Universities, 1983; G. Kurian, 1984; J. L'Esperance, 1983; P.L. McGrath, 1976; P. Robertson, 1982; D. Robins-Mowry, 1983; A. Rossi and A. Calderwood, 1973; R.L. Sivard, 1985; UN Decade for Women, **(C) Education**, 1984; UNESCO, **Tendances**, 1984; UNICEF, **Situation in Kenya**, 1985; UN World Conference for Women, **Review and Evaluation: Education**, 1980, and **Statistical Abstract**, 1980; US Department of Commerce, Census, **Women in the World: Latin America and the Caribbean**, 1984; Urquhart and Buckley, 1965.

24 WORDS FOR WOMEN

The official UNESCO definition of literacy is 'the ability to read and write a sentence in daily life'. Using this definition, most industrialized countries report illiteracy rates of near nought per cent. This clearly ignores the problem of functional illiteracy, which is a serious and growing problem. Recent estimates in the USA, for example, conclude that 16 per cent of all whites, 44 per cent of all blacks, and 56 per cent of all Hispanics fall into the category of functional illiterates – and that 60 per cent of these are women.

There is a lot of international data on literacy rates, but illiteracy is also known to be widely under-reported – and underestimation usually means that information on women is more masked than that on men. It is generally safe to assume that illiteracy – and especially women's illiteracy – is a bigger problem than official statistics reveal.

The *gap* in illiteracy between men and women (not just absolute literacy rates) reveals the most about the relative burden of illiteracy borne by women. The map shows both indicators. In many countries few girls or boys go to school, and illiteracy for both runs high. But as adults, men have more opportunities than women to learn to read and write. Domestic duties and restrictive presumptions about women's roles often keep women too busy in, and confined to, the home for participation in adult literacy programmes. If literacy programmes are to help women, they must be designed for them.

There is little disagreement that literacy is a 'good thing', and that full literacy for all is an important social goal. However, some literacy programmes can be quite damaging – especially in countries with multiple languages and ethnic divisions. In many instances, ethnic children are taught in only one language, in an effort by the State to undermine ethnic identity. In other instances, certain groups have been excluded from the language of power; this is especially true of women. In Latin America, for example, more Indian men than women speak Spanish, and thus are better equipped to participate in national politics and power struggles.

Sources: K. Kelley, 1985; J.L. Scherer, 1983 and 1984; UN, **Compendium**, 1977; UN World Conference for Women, Statistical Abstract, 1985; UNESCO, **Statistical Yearbook**, 1983.

---

25 BREAD AND WATER

Fatigue is the most common chronic health problem for women. A male doctor in Mexico is quoted by Perdita Huston, 'Anaemia in women is extremely high. I don't really understand how they keep going'.

Anaemia is caused primarily by malnutrition. Half of all women, and two-thirds of all pregnant women in poor countries (not including China), suffer from iron-deficiency anaemia. It can be a mild condition, but does lead to higher maternal mortality and morbidity and a lowered work capacity. Anaemia affects women (and children) most because of their higher requirements for iron, in combination with their inadequate intake. Continuous childbearing and infection also contribute.

Women eat less and last, men and children are served first and best. It is estimated that there is a 42 per cent gap between the daily calorie requirement and actual daily calorie intake for women in India). Food taboos (for example no eggs during pregnancy for fear of developing a large foetus and having a painful birth) contribute to female malnutrition. Generally it is thought that women do not need – or deserve – as much food as others. The low birth weight of a mother's baby is an accurate reflection of her own poor physical condition.

Hard work, childbearing, and too little food cause anaemia; but 80 per cent of all disease in poor countries is caused by contaminated water. A billion people in the world lack safe drinking water; including 25 per cent of all city-dwellers and 71 per cent of urban-dwellers.

Sources: P. Blair, 1981; W.U. Chandler, 1984; PAHO, **Health Conditions**, 1982; E. Royston, 1982; UN Decade for Women, **Selected Statistics**, 1985; UNICEF, **State of World's Children, 1984**; WHO, **Prevalence of Anemia in Women**, 1979.

---

26 ILLNESS AND HEALTH

Women contribute most of the world's informal health care – far exceeding that given in the formal medical sector. Yet their own health needs have often been neglected or ignored by health planners.

Primary health care – local-level, semi-professional, preventative and low cost – is the key to improving the health of women around the world. Extending it to everyone in the world would cost $US 10 billion annually, one-twenty-fifth as much as the world spends on cigarettes. Nevertheless, this would represent a doubling of health expenditures for some countries.

As it is, public health spending priorities are skewed towards the inappropriate technology of the modern urban hospital, to which women seldom have access (figures from UNICEF).

Health expenditures and population served	Poor countries	
	(percentage of national health budgets)	(percentage of population)
PHC	15	90
Hospital care	85	10

Sources: American Cancer Society, 1985; P. Blair, 1981; W.U. Chandler, 1984; **The Economist**, 23 February 1985; S. Okie, 1985; personal communication from National Cancer Institute, USA; C. Russell, 1985; **Science News**, 17 April 1982; UN Decade for Women, **Selected Statistics**, 1985, and State of World's Women, 1985; UNICEF, **State of World's Children**, 1984.

---

27 REFUGEES

Not only do women comprise the majority of refugees, but they also suffer greater hardships *as* refugees. Women as refugees are still expected to perform the tasks of childcare, cleaning, cooking and collecting fuel and water, but often without resources. Family survival depends on women's ability to adjust and compensate for impoverishment. Women also suffer considerable abuse. Rape by camp guards, border guards, and other refugees is all too common; the most publicized case of refugee rape is the constant marauding of refugee boats in the China Sea, where it is estimated that over 2400 women have been raped by pirates.

Though about 80 per cent of the world's refugees are women, and women also represent about 80 per cent of health care workers in refugee camps, they have little control over the administration of camps and little voice in the development of national and international refugee policies. Only about one-quarter of the UNHCR budget is earmarked for women's refugee programmes. More generally, women have little influence over the policies that bring about the wars and famines that produce refugees in the first place.

Countries that receive refugees are often in no position to help them. Somalia, for example, is facing drought at the same time that it is hosting over half a million Ethiopian refugees. The ratio of refugees to local population in Somalia is 1 in 7; in the Sudan, the ratio is 1 in 32. Generally, this means that life for refugees is almost as bad in the host country as in the country they fled. When resources are stretched thin, it is women, the most marginalized in the first place, who suffer first and most. Women have the smallest share of the 'resources pie' of the world; when the pie shrinks, women's losses are greatest.

Statistics on international refugees should be treated with caution. In the first place, refugee numbers are very fluid and reporting does not keep pace with fast-changing refugee situations. More important, it is known that refugee reporting is very susceptible to manipulation for political gain. Refugee statistics should be used for the general picture they offer, not the precision.

This map shows international refugees only. Many countries have large internal refugee populations that are as badly off as the international refugees. Cyprus, Angola, El Salvador, Nicaragua, and Guatemala, among others, have very large populations of internal refugees.

Sources: R. Aitchison, 1984; L. Bonnerjea, 1985; M. Kidron & R. Segal, 1984; Minority Rights Group, **Refugee Dilemma**, 1981; UN Decade for Women, **(J) Refugee and Displaced Women**; UNHCR, **Fact Sheets, Refugees**, 1984, 1985, and **World Refugee Map**, 1984; US Committee for Refugees, 1983.

28 POVERTY

Worldwide, the largest poverty groups are, first, women-headed households, and second, the elderly (a greater proportion of whom are women because women live longer than men). Together, these two groups represent on average 70 per cent of the poor in most countries in the world. Poverty is rapidly being feminized. The scattered statistics that are available tell the same story worldwide: in the USA, 78 per cent of all people living in poverty are women or children under the age of 18; in Australia, the proportion is 75 per cent; in Canada, 60 per cent of all women over age 65 live in poverty.

The reasons for women-headed households being poor can be found in the maps in the 'Work' section (Maps 15 through 20). Women who are solely responsible for their families often cannot go out to work because there are no childcare facilities available (or because childcare is too expensive). When women do work for wages, they get paid less, they are ghettoized into low-paying jobs with little job security, and have fewer job benefits. In agricultural economies, credit, money and land ownership are often denied women (see Map 21, 'Access to Means'); women are dependent on men for access to the resources and rewards of the formal economy. In the absence of men, women are cut off from access to resources.

There are great income differences between women-headed and men-headed households. In 1981 in the USA, the average income of women-headed households was $US 10,960; for men-headed households, it was $US 19,889; for husband-wife households, it was $US 25,065. In Chile 29 per cent of women-headed households fall into the lowest income bracket, compared with 10 per cent of men-headed households.

Recessions and other economic hardships strike hardest at those with the least income: women and their children feel 'hard times' first and most. The poorer a family is, the larger is the proportion of income spent on necessities, such as food, fuel and health care. For poor families, then, any decline in income threatens survival.

The poorer women are, the more vulnerable they are to exploitation, especially prostitution. There is a very strong connection between women's poverty and prostitution.

The number of women-headed households is everywhere increasing rapidly. In rich countries divorce is the major cause of the rise in single-parent families (see Map 5, 'Single States'); in poor countries, it is due to both divorce and the migration (either seasonal or permanent) of men seeking work.

Sources: N. Banerjee, 1983; M. Buvinic, 1978; D. Dwyer, 1983; ILO, **Women at Work**, various issues; J. Massiah, 1983; R. Morgan, 1984; PRB, 'The changing American family', 1983; press reports; J. Schirmer, 1982; H. Scott, 1984; K. Stallard et al., 1983; UNICEF, **Assignment Children**, Spring 1980, and **The State of the World's Children 1985**; UN World Assembly on Aging, 1982; US Commission on Civil Rights, 1983; US Department of Commerce, **Women of the World: A Chartbook**, 1985; US Department of Labor, 'Time of change', 1984; **WIN News**, Summer 1985.

29 THE VOTE

Women are still not fully enfranchised worldwide. Despite growing protests, the Kuwaiti government refuses to grant women the vote; in a 1985 debate, the

Interpretation Committee of Kuwait's Ministry of Islamic Affairs concluded that, 'the nature of the electoral process befits men, who are endowed with ability and expertise: it is not permissible that women nominate women or men'. In Bhutan, a 'one vote per family' rule means that men almost exclusively claim that right. Hong Kong has property restrictions that prevent some men, and a lot of women, from voting. And in South Africa, black women and men are still denied the vote.

The biggest surge in voting rights came during the late 1950s – in the wake of decolonization. But in many countries women's suffrage is even more recent: in Lichtenstein, women only won the vote in 1984; in Jordan, it was in 1982.

Partly because women do not have such a long history of political participation they tend to vote less than men. In many countries, and in many families, there is little encouragement for women to act autonomously and politically.

When women do vote, they increasingly vote differently than men on certain issues. These differences in political attitudes first began to be noticed consistently in the mid-1970s in American elections. The 'gender gap' at the polls has since become an important factor in elections in the USA. Women's voting records show that they are more likely to favour stronger environmental protection regulation, gun control, abolition of the death penalty, and are more likely to vote against weapons build-ups.

Historical information on women's suffrage is often hard to interpret. In many cases there is simply no record in standard historical sources. More often the dates in various sources are conflicting. This is because in many countries *some* women had the vote before others – and different sources record different benchmarks. For this map, we mark suffrage from the date that *all* women won the vote on equal terms with each other and on equal terms with men.

Sources: S. Baxter & M. Lansing, 1983; D. Boulding, 1976; D. Butler et al., 1981; CEC, **European Women and Men**, 1983; Minority Rights Group, **Latin American Women**, 1983; National Commission on Working Women, 1984; UN Commission on the Status of Women (annual reports); US Department of State, **Reports** (various), 1984.

30 GOVERNMENT

The importance of women's recent gains in political power must be measured against the fact that even in the best cases women represent only about 25 per cent of elected national officials. In many countries women have *no* share of political power. This is certainly true in all countries ruled by militaries (since women are nowhere in power in militaries – see Map 32, 'Military Service'), and in many countries where women only recently won the vote. Lichtenstein, for example, has only one woman member of parliament, elected in 1986.

A widespread pattern shows women to have made some gains in lower levels of legislature, but to the excluded from the upper echelons where real power lies. The most obvious example of this is in the Eastern European countries:

Number of women in Politburos, 1985

Bulgaria	0	Romania	1
China	1	USSR	0
Czechoslovakia	0	Vietnam	0
E. Germany	0	Yugoslavia	1
Poland	1		

When women do hold cabinet posts, they are often appointments in areas considered to lie within women's traditional interests – not considered to be very serious: women get appointed to be Ministers of Consumer Affairs, not Ministers of Defence. There are many countries where no woman has yet made it to the level of a cabinet position.

Women tend to fare better in local politics. They typically have better representation in municipal councils than in national bodies. In the national legislatures in Scandinavian countries, women had achieved over 20 per cent representation by the early 1970s. They remain in the lead today. The 1985 figures are: Denmark, 26 per cent; Finland, 31 per cent; Norway, 26 per cent; and Sweden, 29 per cent.

Data on women in government is generally reliable, and coverage is fairly good – but a surprising number of countries still do not collect or report data on this topic.

Sources: AFSC, 1984; G. Flanz, 1983; J. Lovenduski & J. Hills, 1981; J. & K. Macksey, 1975; M. Shaul, 1982; R.L. Sivard, 1985; UNECA, **Mozambique**, 1980; UN World Conference for Women, **Report**, 1980; **Women of Europe**, March 1984.

31 THE LAW

Cross-cultural data on crime must be treated with caution. For one thing, there is considerable variation in what type of behaviour is defined as 'criminal' – and definitions change over time. In addition, there is little uniformity in national governments' methods of reporting their 'crime rate' to international authorities: in some instances anyone who is arrested is listed as a 'criminal'; in other countries 'criminals' are those *convicted* of crimes. On this map the crime rate is based on arrest records.

In addition to these interpretation problems there are major gaps in international data on the law and its enforcement. Very little information is broken down according to gender. For example, while there is some data on reported crimes, there is no information on women as political prisoners. (Amnesty International, which is the primary group monitoring political prisoners, does not collect information by sex.) There is little information on women in police forces, though in the USA women reportedly comprise six per cent of police forces nationwide.

The little information that exists on women in prisons suggests that overall they comprise a very small proportion of inmates. In Pakistan women are less than one per cent of all prison inmates; in Sweden, two per cent; in the Netherlands and the UK, three per cent; in China, five per cent. Contrary to commonly held beliefs, women do not get off lightly in the courts: a 1975 study in the UK showed that five times as many women with no previous convictions were jailed as men with no previous convictions.

Women are a small but growing proportion of lawyers and judges. Here, too, job ghettoization exists. Women judges are much more likely than men to be appointed to family courts. Very few women rise to posts in the upper courts.

Sources: F. Adler, 1981; Change International Reports, various countries; Interpol, 1979-80; G. Kurian, 1984; R. Morgan, 1984; New York Times, 10 March 1985; Pakistan, Ministry of Information and Broadcasting, 1981; Statistics Sweden, 1985; US Department of Justice, 1983; WIN News, various issues; Women of Europe, various issues.

32 MILITARY SERVICE

All over the world, there is controversy about whether women should be allowed to participate in militaries – and if so, to what extent. In some countries women are completely excluded from military service; in others, women can join the military, but are restricted to the lowest levels in the power hierarchy and slotted into typically 'feminized' jobs.

Notions of femininity are at the centre of all arguments against allowing women into the military. Women are portrayed as a weaker species who must be protected – indeed, men are encouraged to fight for their country in order to 'protect' women. The idea of women serving in the military, then, is discordant with the ideals of behaviour for both men and women: women shouldn't be in the military because it is unfeminine, and because it undermines the rationales used to keep men as soldiers. The idea of women being allowed to serve in *combat* is considered to be even further beyond the pale. Ideologies about femininity and the inappropriateness of women in the military are virtually universal: the same arguments are used by revolutionary governments, Communist governments, free market governments, in rich countries and poor.

Among feminists, too, the issue of whether women should be in the military is controversial; much of the feminist debate focuses specifically on conscription. In some countries, women argue *against* the conscription of women on the grounds that they should not be compelled to join male institutions of violence; there has been strong anti-conscription rallying in Italy, Greece, East and West Germany, and the USA. Increasingly European governments facing a decline in military manpower are considering the conscription of women. Yet in other countries women have argued on the basis of equal rights that they *should* be conscripted. For example, the recent decision of the Nicaraguan government not to conscript women was taken by many women as a snub, given their service in combat in the struggle to overthrow Somoza.

When women do break into the ranks, they are usually confined to 'women's roles', which (as in society at large) tend to be the least skilled, the lowest paid and have the least potential for promotion. Most militaries use women to provide 'support services', as nurses, secretaries and communications aides.

It is generally true that military service brings some social and economic benefits; by excluding women from service, they are excluded from these benefits too. In many countries, the military is the goverment – which means that the government is exclusively male, and women are held at a great distance from power.

Sources: C. Enloe, 1983, and conversations with C. Enloe; N.L. Goldman, 1982; Les Femmes et L'Armée, 1981; Minerva (quarterly); Minority Rights Group, Latin American Women, 1983; R. Morgan, 1984; NATO, 1984; S. Urdag, 1984; Women of Europe, various issues.

33 BODY AND MIND

The status of women in the health and education professions reflects an observation made by Margaret Mead about men's work and women's work: 'There are villages in which men fish and women weave, and those in which women fish and men weave, but in either type of village, the work done by men is valued higher than the work done by women.' In both health and education, the ranks with the greatest numbers of women – nursing and pre-primary school education – have the lowest status.

In most countries more than 90 per cent of nurses are women. In a few places, such as the UK and the USA, the proportion of male nurses is slowly increasing. And when this happens, the men rise to the top: although they are a minority of all nurses, they hold a disproportionate share of senior nursing posts – and nursing unions and organizations are generally dominated by the few men in them. In a few countries severe restrictions imposed on women's education and their activities outside the home has meant that nursing has never been feminized.

The proportion of women doctors worldwide has been rising steadily since World War Two, with the greatest increases appearing in the Communist countries – this is the result of a deliberate policy, and now in some parts of Eastern Europe the majority of doctors are women.

Many countries, notably in Europe and the USA, fail to report educational staff data to UNESCO, the only agency that keeps track of this information internationally. Thus on the education 'ladders' graphic there are some surprising countries for which the data is listed as 'unknown' – entirely the result of national policy on reporting to the UN.

Information on the proportion of women in the various parts of the health professions is surprisingly hard to find. The World Health Organization does not collect or report this data (with the exception of one listing made in 1977). Although it would seem an easy task to collect information on women as nurses and doctors (since health professionals everywhere are registered with the national health authorities), we were told by WHO that this information was 'not considered important to collect'.

Information on the important role of women as primary health-care providers is included on several maps, especially Map 11, 'Birth Care'.

Sources: Bui Dang Ha Doan, 1979; International Council of Nurses, 1983; G. Lapidus, 1978; R. Morgan, 1984; J. Salvage, 1985; Statistical Abstract of Latin America, 1982; State Statistical Bureau, China, 1984; UN, Compendium, 1980; UN Decade for Women, Selected Statistics, 1985; UNESCO, Statistical Yearbook, 1981, 1983; US Department of Commerce, Statistical Abstract, 1984; WHO, World Health Statistics, 1983;

34 THE MEDIA

In the USA there is only one mass-media magazine owned and operated by women (Ms.). So-called 'women's' magazines are owned by men, almost always published by men, and usually edited by men. By contrast, all the feminist print media listed in 'The Furthest Reach' graphic are owned and operated by women. Not surprisingly the sex magazines are owned and operated almost completely by men.

At their best, 'women's magazines' provide a wealth of practical information; at their worst they aggressively reinforce what is most negative about traditional notions of femininity. It matters; 29,500,000 people received the magazines listed in the 'Reach' graphic alone. Compare this with the 943,000 recipients of the feminist magazines and the 13.8 million pornography readers listed.

Much of the pornography industry is outside the regular economy and thus is hard to document. Figures used to estimate its size are thought to be very low (the US industry is estimated as $US 8 billion in 1984). The industry barely existed before the 1960s, but its growth since then has been explosive. There are well over 165 pornographic magazines in the USA alone and their content is increasingly violent and explicit, and the women featured continue to be exploited. One issue of *Penthouse* magazine featuring old photographs of the then-Miss America sold 10 million copies, netted the publisher $US 37 million and Miss America nothing but the loss of her crown for unbecoming behaviour. A content analysis of pornographic paperbacks found that depictions of rape had doubled between 1968 and 1974; depictions of bondage and domination have also increased dramatically. Pornography is anathema because it dehumanizes people; it has nothing to do with healthy adult sexuality.

For many women, especially the millions of poor and illiterate women, print media is irrelevant to their lives. Radio is the most accessible of all the media; in Europe and parts of Africa, for example, more women listen to radio than do men.

Sources: M.L. Allen, 1985; E.L. Anani, 1981; Austrian Federal Ministry (n.d.); B.H. Bagdikian, 1983; S. Brownmiller, 1975; CEC, Women of Europe, various issues; Clearinghouse on Development Communication, 1983; Consumers Association of Penang, 1982; G.F. Epstein & R. L. Coser, 1984; M. Gallagher, 1981; J. Gay, 1983; IMS/Ayer, 1985; ISIS, 'Women and the media', 1981, and 'Women and visual images', 1983; J. Koten & R. Johnson, 1985; L. Lederer, 1980; Media Development, 1984; R. Morgan, 1984; K. Newland, 1979; Pakistan, Ministry of Information and Broadcasting, 1982; NOW, 1984; S. Pervaiz (n.d.); D.E. Russell, 1982; Ulrich's International, 1985; US News and World Report (weekly).

35 BEAUTY BEAT

In addition to the two major international contests, hundreds of beauty contests are held around the world each year. Contests present women and 'beauty' as commodities – and are in this way directly related to the images of women presented in pornography and in the mass media. A wide range of countries participate in the beauty beat. Ideologies of beauty – and of women as objects of beauty – transcend all sorts of other political and economic differences. The beauty beat seems to be gathering momentum. Beauty contests were begun in China in 1985; Hungary also started to hold contests in 1985; in 1983 Poland was the first Eastern bloc country to send a contestant to Miss World. Muslim countries are the only ones that do not host beauty contests.

Although beauty contests are supposed to be non-political 'entertainment', they are at the centre of much controversy and acrimony. Feminists uniformly condemn beauty contests. Criticism is also more widespread – for example in 1984 the BBC ended coverage of beauty contests, calling them 'anachronistic and offensive'. Hosting a pageant can be very controversial – especially in poorer countries, since governments spend a lot of money preparing sites and promoting contests held in their country; the sites of beauty contests are almost always the sites of protests. Most contests are riven with internal contradictions: there is always a furore, for example, when it is discovered that one of the contestants has posed nude for modelling or pornography magazines, or that one of the contestants had a teenage pregnancy. Every year there are a number of beauty queens deposed for one transgression or another.

A staggering amount of money and suffering is spent on the pursuit of beauty. Some cosmetic surgery is essential – reconstruction following surgery, for example. But the overwhelming proportion of cosmetic surgery is non-essential, and indicates the extent to which women have been socialized to pursue the elusive ideal of beauty at any cost.

Sources: Christian Science Monitor, 20 March 1984; **Drug and Cosmetic Industry**, various issues; **Forbes**, 18 June 1984; Miss Universe, 1985; Miss World, 1985; **Newsweek**, 'Health supplement', Fall 1985; R. Stern, 1982.

36 SEX FOR SALE

Prostitution is as old as patriarchy. Prostitution flourishes in an economic context where women are paid less than men for their labour power, and the one commodity they possess for which men are willing to pay a price is their bodies. Prostitution exists everywhere. But to say simply that it 'exists' masks the processes through which prostitution is perpetuated – economic processes, male networks of control and trade in women, and the violence and coercion that permeates all systems of prostitution.

International traffic in women is flourishing; trafficking means simply the transport, exchange, and sale of women through networks set up and controlled by men. Most trafficking takes one of three forms. Firstly, women who are already prostitutes in one country are often 'exchanged' to another country. Since most prostitutes are in the control of pimps, they have no say in these transfers – they are merely commodities being exchanged between men. Secondly, girls are often sold into prostitution by poor families; the families are in some instances aware that they are selling their daughter into prostitution, but more often than not they are told that the child will be employed as a domestic servant in a patron's home. Once prostituted, the already low value of girls to their families drops even lower. Thirdly, there is evidence of women being recruited from poverty under false pretences – they are hired to be 'waitresses' or 'domestic servants', and are then forced into prostitution. Much of the international traffic in women takes the form of sexual slavery.

Marriage bureaux which offer women for sale to prospective husbands – a supposedly legitimate business – are often little more than fronts for prostitute networks. Women bought through these marriage brokers are often put to work as prostitutes in foreign countries. Even when marriage bureaux do not serve to supply prostitute networks, the fact that they are established in order to sell women closely relates them to the business of prostitution.

Sex tourism is literally that: hundred of thousands of men each year flock to various centres in Southeast Asia for 'sex holidays'. Tours are arranged by 'legitimate' travel operators in Japan, West Germany and Scandinavia, who for one all-in price offer airfare, a hotel room and a pre-arranged number of women 'for the men to do as they like with'. The women who are offered up for these sex tours are often kept in conditions of near-slavery, and one common practice is to parade women with numbers around their necks through hotel viewing rooms so the men can pick whom they want. Many of the prostitutes are children: there are an estimated 30,000 prostitutes in Bangkok under the age of 16, for example. Sex tourism is big business, and in most instances has the implicit (or even direct) support of the host government: sex tourism is a major source of foreign currency and, in many cases, props up a failing economy. Sex tourism in many countries started with brothels established to service military bases.

Prostitution and/or related activities are illegal in most countries. Even where prostitution itself is technically not a crime, it is always the prostitutes – not the pimps or customers – who are harassed or arrested. Nowhere is there legal protection for prostitutes, nor prosecution of the men who exploit prostitutes.

Sources; Asian Women's Association, 1980; K. Barry, 1984; conversations with K. Barry; K. Barry, C. Bunch & S. Castley, 1984; Canadian Advisory Council, 1984; **Connexions**, various issues; ISIS 'Prostitution: who pays?', 1984; R. Morgan, 1984; **New York Times**, 24 June 1985; V. Ohse, 1984; P. Phongpaichit, 1982; **Spare Rib**, Oct 1985; K. Thitsa, 1980; UN Economic and Social Council, 1982 and 1983; **Washington Post**, 3 March 1985; **Women in Europe**, various issues.

37 RAPE

Rape is not uncontrolled lust and it is not 'having sex'. Rape is a violent act done by a man to a woman – sometimes to a child – in order to establish power over her or women in general. It is committed mostly when and where men can get away with it – often in the home – and without regard to a woman's age or appearance. It is not true that most rapes are committed by strangers, only on pretty women, when the woman is 'asking for it'. If a woman fights back she may be seriously injured or killed; but if she doesn't, she is assumed to have been complicit in the act. This puts women in a no-win situation. Because some men rape, all women are threatened by rape and are thus unable to move about freely.

Rape is not an impulse act in most cases. In the USA one study showed 90 per cent of gang rapes, 83 per cent of pair rapes and 58 per cent of single rapes to be premeditated. Most cultures either condone rape or legitimize it by ignoring it in reality and enjoying it in fantasy. As some feminists say, 'Pornography is the theory, rape is the practice'. The 'ideal' woman in the media's image is very similar to the 'ideal' rape victim: docile, selfless, a sex object.

The Dublin rape crisis centre in Ireland experienced a two-fold increase in women seeking help between 1983 and 1984. As rape rates and reporting increase, pressure by women's groups is forcing legal systems to respond to rape as a serious social problem. In many countries, however, the legal system *is* part of the problem. Institutional rape by jail guards and police in prisons, by 'orderlies' in mental hospitals, by authorities in refugee camps (see Notes to Map 27, 'Refugees'), is used to remind women of their powerlessness and to keep them powerless. It is also used by men against other men, as in war: the conquering soldier rapes and plunders to establish his dominance over his counterpart through property. Where rape *is* severely punished, as in Muslim countries, the crime is seen as an affront to the possessing male, not to the woman victim. In every case the punishment of rape is contingent on its being reported, which in turn is contingent upon a woman being able to recognize rape as the unjustifiable assault it is, not something deserved – particularly as in wife-rape or 'date-rape'. Men and women still assume on some level that the rape victim is guilty of enticement or some other attitude which legitimately provokes a man to rape. Women hesitate to report rape for other reasons, too: fear of reprisal from her attacker or his compatriots and lack of faith in the criminal justice system which might put *her* on trial for *her* sexuality. In the USA ten rapes are reported every hour. This probably represents – at a conservative estimate – ten per cent of those occurring.

Historically the criminalization of rape was not designed to protect women but to protect male property. The rape of a man's wife or daughter was and is considered a serious crime; wife-as-property lingers as a category in the law. This is evident in the recent and still rare acceptance of wife-rape as prosecutable. (You cannot violate the rights of someone who – in your mind or in the law – has no independent civil rights of her own.) Some countries only recognize wife-rape when a husband and wife are *separated*, thereby failing to accept the basic concept. Canada and Yugoslavia are examples. In general socialist law protects wives from rape most, Muslim law the least. The insistence by some on calling wife-rape 'spousal rape' begs the issue, which is most certainly *not* gender-neutral.

Because rape is so under-reported, statistics are unreliable. This is as true of small-sample studies as it is of Interpol statistics. There is extreme hesitancy on the part of women to report rape, and a certain lack of determination by authorities to collect accurate numbers. The definition of 'sex offences' varies widely too. The 'sex offence' figure for the USA includes only rape, while in other countries, prostitution, the traffic in women and other crimes are included. It is thus difficult to make any generalizations about cultural patterns based on these statistics.

Sources: S. Brownmiller, 1975; A.W. Burgess, 1985; Canadian Advisory Council, 'Sexual assault', 1985; M. Capuzzo, 1984; Interpol, 1979-80; ISIS, 'Organizing against Rape', 1979; G. Kurian, 1984; M.A. Largen, 1985; London Rape Crisis Centre; J. Mann, 1985; **Newsweek**, 1985; **New York Times**, 29 December 1984; **Off Our Backs**, Aug/Sept, 1984; D.E. Russell, 1982; D.E. Russell & N. Van der Ven, 1984; US Department of Justice, 1983; WAP, 1985; **Washington Post**, 20 August 1985; H. Wheeler, 1985; **WIN News** (quarterly); Women's History Resource Centre; K. Yllo and D. Finkelhor, 1985.

38 CHANNELS OF CHANGE

Women have created powerful channels of change over the past decade. The women's non-governmental organizations (NGOs) took key roles in forging resolutions and recommendations at the three UN Decade of Women conferences. In most countries women's political action groups have become important lobbying forces. Women's research centres have been founded in more than 25 countries.

They have fared less well inside conventional channels. Only a few governments have established women's ministries – and in some (for example Canada), the minister is a man. Women are not represented in senior posts or policy-making positions within any of the major international agencies.

In most countries women have been forming professional and political organizations since the mid-19th century. Suffrage organizations began in the 1860s in England and the USA, and in the 1880s and 1990s in the Scandinavian countries. Some of the earliest international women's organizations were created around peace issues. A note of irony is that in some women's organizations, men hold the top posts: the

League of Women Voters (US) for example, founded in 1920, just elected – in 1986 – a man as its executive director.

Sources: E. Boulding, 1977, and 1980; G.F. Epstein & R. L. Coser, 1984; R.J. Evans, 1977; ILO, **Women at Work**, Vol. 1, 1984; International Women's Tribune Centre, 'Women's centers', 1982; ISIS, **Women in Development**, 1983; **New York Times**, 11 September 1985; UN, **Report of the World Conference**, 1975; UN Decade for Women, **Report of the Secretary-General**, 1985, and **Report of the World Conference**, 1985, UN World Conference for Women, **Descriptive List**, 1980, and **Report**, 1980; US Congress, **Women in Development**, 1984.

39 PROTESTS

Women's protests are not new – women have always struggled against their oppression. Contemporary movements have links back to early women textile-workers' strikes, and prohibition and temperance movements.

Many women's street demonstrations have been called to protest for reproductive rights and legal equality, and against male violence. Recently, in the Arab states women have organized against repressive 'Family Codes'. In Iceland women organized a one-day strike (in 1975 and again in 1985) against 'male privilege'.

The list of street demonstrations was gleaned from the back-issues of several feminist magazines and newspaper indexes – but we know it is not complete. We have not mapped the various and numerous 'Take Back the Night' marches that have occurred throughout Europe, Australia, Canada, and the USA.

Sources: Connexions (quarterly); R. Kamel, 1985; R. Morgan, 1984; **New Internationalist**, various issues; New Internationalist, **Women: A World Report**, 1985; Puget Sound Women's Peace Camp, 1985; **Spare Rib**, various issues; **Women's Peace Alliance**, June 1985.

40 MAPPING THE PATRIARCHY

The collection and dissemination of statistics about people is political. The collecting agency must decide how, where and why to collect information, and what it should be. These choices are made, by and large, by men. As a result women are often absent from compendia of international statistics. Where information on women is included it is often incomplete and concerns either what the collectors consider important about women or what is most easily obtained. (It is also true that certain information about men – for example men as fathers – is not collected.)

The lack of data on issues of concern to women certainly frustrates researchers, but its implications go far beyond that. Decisions affecting millions of people – as in international development planning – hinge on the nature of the information used by the decision-makers. The failure to recognize that women are half the labour force, all of the reproducing force and almost all of the food preparation force – among other things – has contributed to failure of many development schemes' by effectively keeping out of the picture half of the society supposedly being helped.

Sources: E. Boulding, 1976; IPPF wallchart, 1985; B. Rogers, 1980; UN Decade for Women, **(B) Health and Nutrition**, 1984, and **Selected Statistics** 1985; USAID, 1984.